The direct, synergistic style of Easum (consummate trainer) and Cornelius (zealous learner) will ignite sparks among your leadership team. Bill and Bil have each raised the bar for multiplying disciples and leaders in their respective generations. . . . The remarkably similar perspectives of these two catalytic leaders transcend regional culture and multiple generations. While contextually aware, *Go BIG* beautifully distills timeless passions, principles, and practices to help churches thrive almost anywhere."

—Dan Reeves, Institute for Missional Leadership Teams

"Instead of constantly making excuses about why we aren't growing, Easum and Cornelius challenge us to look at ourselves as leaders, and urge us to follow the Great Commission to be what the church is meant to be. Although we may not always agree, this book is a must-read for any local church pastor."

—Linda S. McCoy, author of *Planting a Garden: Growing the Church Beyond Traditional Models*

"*Go BIG* is a BIG-time book! It's authored by a BIG-time church planter and a BIG-time consultant who boldly tell us about a BIG God who is doing BIG things and wants to do even BIGGER things in your church! I love *Go BIG* because it tells the truth that BIG is not bad and then teaches us how BIG can accomplish the Jesus mission in our churches. So, if you want familiar-stagnant-small-little-decline, leave this book on the shelf. But if you want crazy-go-BIG-huge-growth then pick up *Go BIG* now!"

—Dave Ferguson, Community Christian Church / NewThing Network

---

"These are the type of leaders we need to help us think about how best to reach those far from the church and the gospel. Too many experts lack passion and wisdom; in this book you find ample helpings of both."

—Ed Stetzer, Missiologist and author of *Breaking the Missional Code*

"*Go BIG: Lead Your Church to Explosive Growth* is a straight-talking, faith-building, fear-stomping, Kingdom-expanding, denial-busting, adrenaline-pumping book!

—Jorge Acevedo, Pastor of Grace Church, Cape Coral, Florida

"This book is courageous, insightful, and helpful to any pastor. Its bold recommendations contradict what most of the experts are saying about such things as the emerging nature of the church and team-based leadership because, as usual, the experts are wrong."

—Mark Driscoll, Founding Pastor of Mars Hill Church, Seattle

"*Go BIG* will inspire pastors to dream again, to strive for their vision, to find a way forward that overcomes fear, pessimism, or cynicism."

—Todd Hunter, National Director, Alpha U.S.A.

"Bill continues to stay on the edge of what God's doing in the Church. He is one of the best at giving direction to church leaders for tomorrow."

—Mike Slaughter, Lead Pastor of Ginghamsburg Church, Tipp City, Ohio

Lead Your Church
to Explosive Growth

BILL EASUM
BIL CORNELIUS

ABINGDON PRESS / Nashville

GO BIG
LEAD YOUR CHURCH TO EXPLOSIVE GROWTH

Copyright © 2006 by Abingdon Press

This book is printed on acid-free paper.

Library of Congress Cataloging-in-Publication Data

Easum, William M., 1939-
    Go big : lead your church to explosive growth / Bill Easum and Bil Cornelius.
        p. cm.
    ISBN 0-687-33442-X (binding: adhesive, pbk. : alk. paper)
    1. Church growth.   I. Cornelius, Bil, 1972-   II. Title.

    BV652.25.E38 2006
    254'.5—dc22
                                                            2006001758

ISBN 13: 978-0-687-33442-1

07 08 09 10 11 12 13 14 15—10 9 8 7 6 5 4 3 2

MANUFACTURED IN THE UNITED STATES OF AMERICA

CONTENTS

FOREWORD

The local church is the greatest thing going and growing. That's one of my favorite statements. I say it and spray it everywhere I go, because I believe so strongly that the church should always be on the move. It should constantly be going and growing; the reverse—stagnant and dying—is an unacceptable condition for the body of Christ.

This book is a reflection of that powerful reality. Bil Cornelius and Bill Easum inspire us to dream big for Christ and his church! They do a great job addressing the challenges and excitement of leading the local church toward change and growth. I truly believe that church leadership is the most difficult task on the leadership spectrum. Nothing requires more commitment, tenacity, or faith. As pastors, we are called to present the magnetic bride of Christ to a dark and lonely world. This huge challenge requires a tenacious commitment to God's unchanging truth, coupled with a constant read on the pulse of our culture. We must never be afraid to change our methods as we search for new ways to present the "old, old story."

I've had the privilege of getting to know Bil Cornelius during the past several years. In that time, I've been genuinely impressed with his passion for the church. Bil is a man who is firmly committed to creativity, and is constantly challenging me with good questions as he wrestles with various leadership issues related to his church in Corpus Christi. He is an up-and-coming leader who is an inspiration and example to young pastors wanting to plant a healthy and dynamic church. I knew Bill Easum was a great man as soon as I met him because like me, he's a fisherman. He fishes for big-game fish, but also, as a follower of Jesus, Bill is a fisher of men.

Bil and Bill write not just for the reality of the megachurch (though Bil's church now reaches 4,000 each weekend) but also for every leader on the church leadership journey. Because Bil started with only a few people, you'll have the opportunity to trace God's blessings on Bay Area Fellowship through their various stages of growth. You'll also benefit greatly by the seasoned wisdom of Bill Easum, a sought-after church consultant who has gleaned incredible insight from his thirty years in the trenches of leadership and through his research of contemporary church issues.

I know these authors will infect you with their enthusiasm for the Lord and his church. They will challenge you to ask the right questions about your own leadership situation and will equip you with the raw answers you need to go BIG for God.

Ed Young
Senior Pastor
Fellowship Church, Grapevine, Texas
Author, *The Creative Leader*

INTRODUCTION

GET READY FOR A RIDE

We begin with a story. A story designed to whet your appetite for what BIG things God can do through those who dream BIG and act on those dreams. We want to help you learn how to dream BIG. So, we tell our story up front so it can be the foundation for your BIG dream.

"I've always found that God is seldom at the forefront of what is possible. If it's possible, we don't need God. However, I've always found God in the impossible."

—Bill Easum

The two authors of this story are Bil Cornelius and Bill Easum. We're not trying to confuse you, Bil just doesn't know how to spell his name. In most places we will tell this story in one voice but when necessary, we will note the different voice for you.

Our stories are very similar, yet very different. At the age of twenty-six Bil C. founded Bay Area Fellowship Church. At the age of twenty-nine Bill E. restarted a dead mainline church. Both of us are considered by most church leaders to be extremely successful as pastors.

It is at this point that our stories differ. Bil C. started Bay Area Fellowship in the postmodern world, outside of the mainstream of traditional Christianity. Bill E. restarted Colonial Hills Church in the last gasp of modernity within the mainstream of traditional Christianity. By the age of thirty-two Bil C. was the pastor of some 4,000 plus people on Sunday morning. By the same age Bill E. was the pastor of 500 people on Sunday morning. However, that's not the real story.

When Bill E. talked about reaching San Antonio for Christ, he was met by his peers with "All he is interested in is numbers," and when people viewed his success they often replied "He must be watering down the gospel." When Bil C. talks about reaching Corpus for Christ, his peers and people ask, "Is that all we want to reach? What about other cities? Can't we reach them also?"

The environment of traditional mainstream Protestantism from the 1960s through the end of the twentieth century was one of skepticism, survival, and small dreams. For many in leadership the goal was merely to hold on to what they had, and not decline any more. Bill E. had to continually fight against that mentality. Bil C. was constantly cheered on to bigger dreams by his peers. However, Bil C. found resistance to his dream with the churches of modernity around him.

When Bil C. feels led by God to implement a new idea or ministry all he has to do is let the Ministry Leadership Team, of which he is the chair, in on it. Bil C.'s role is clearly to lead the church. No boards or committees or even deacons are there to slow down the process. When Bill E. felt led by God to implement a new idea or ministry, he had to go through at least one committee and then a board. Bill E. had both to motivate and convince the board that his idea was in fact a leading of God.

When Bil C. spoke of the Great Commission, whether it was saving individuals or redeeming a city, people cheered. When Bill E. spoke of the Great Commission, his peers asked, "Is there really just one way to God?"

Herein lies the fundamental difference today between the traditional mainline church of modernity and the emerging church of postmoderntiy (or whatever you want to call it). The emerging church is exploding today for two primary reasons—the people want leaders to lead, and everyone in leadership is passionately sold out to the Great Commission. This is not to say that there is no conflict or individuals do not bring resistance to the vision, but rather the difficulties come at a different stage of the growth for the emerging church, as we will discuss later.

But we can hear the rising chorus of folks who say, "Isn't that too much authority? What if Bil C. does something he ought not to do?" We will answer this question later. Right now we want you to hear something—most tribes within traditional mainstream Protestantism have placed so many checks and balances on their pastoral leadership to keep them from doing something bad to the church that they have almost ensured that nothing good can happen. You can't fulfill the Great Commission with that attitude and structure.

Our desire is for this story and the learning contained within it to inspire and empower you to dream BIG dreams because the God we serve is a really BIG God.

We now begin the story.

CHAPTER ONE

THE ONLY DIFFERENCE IS THE ZEROS

S even years ago, a twenty-six year old showed up on Bill E.'s doorstep. "Hi," he said. "My name is Bil Cornelius. I'm starting a church in Corpus Christi, and I need help."

Bill E.'s first reaction was, "Sure. I've been here before." But after a few minutes with Bil C., it was clear that this was a young Christian in whom it was worth investing some time. And so it was. Seven years later, Bay Area Fellowship has over 4,000 people worshiping on an average weekend and has been involved in four church plants.

> *The problem with most pastors is that they don't dream big enough.*

Corpus Christi is not the most logical place for a Protestant megachurch to emerge. It is a city of slightly over 300,000 with roughly 60 percent of the population Catholic. Yet in seven short years Bay Area Fellowship has become the largest Protestant church in the city.

How It All Began

Bay Area Fellowship began as a dream in the heart of Bil Cornelius. Five people gathered in Bil and Jessica's home for the first meeting, where Bil announced boldly, "We're going to be a church of thousands one day." After every core group meeting he would challenge the group members with this vision, "Bring everyone you can." And they did. The group went from five to ten people. Then the group grew from ten to fifteen people. Fifteen might not sound like a lot, but to Bil it seemed huge.

Before long the group grew to twenty people and moved out of the apartment, traveling from home to home. Soon the homes were too small and the group moved into a small storefront. The momentum was gathering and so was the excitement.

When the group reached twenty-five, Bil said to the group, "Alright guys, here's what we're going to do. We're going to spend every dime we've got. We're going to blow it all in one weekend. Let's launch. And let's do this BIG." A few years later the people in that core group would remember these words and rejoice that they had not discounted them due to their small size.

With that the tiny group rented a school and, using a regional marketing company, sent out 70,000 direct mail pieces to homes, something that no church had done before in Corpus Christi. At the same time Bil challenged the core group to bring in at least ten people—*each!*

We are aware that sending out a direct mail piece in some parts of the country may seem old hat. The point we are making is that in Corpus Christi it had not been done before. The mailing worked because it was a unique mailing piece (often off-the-wall) and it was a unique tactic for the area. So it is incumbent on you as the leader to find whatever will work in your situation. But we encourage you not to blow off direct mail too quickly even if it has been used several times before in your area, because no one throws away a piece of mail without first glancing at it. When they do, they notice the name of the church.

The first Sunday 236 people showed up and Bay Area Fellowship was born. As expected, the next week's attendance dropped to 150 people, but compared to the twenty-five who launched the church, this number appeared awesome to the group!

The church grew from 150 to about 250 people and moved from the elementary school to a junior high for a bigger campus and more parking. Again, the church grew to 400 or 500 people and God opened the door for the church to purchase an old Moose Lodge. It was a piece of junk, but it was their own junk! No longer did the group have to set up and take down each week. Today, it's still junk, but it's a pretty piece of junk.

Over the next three years the church grew an average of 75 percent a year. Today (2005), Bay Area Fellowship averages over 4,000 people and has purchased 100 acres of land and has plans to build an auditorium large enough for it to continue to expand.

Today, the dream of BAF is to commit a million dollars a year to plant ten churches a year, for ten years. And, according to Bil C., it will happen as if it's already a fact.

A Snapshot of Bay Area Fellowship's Growth

- *1998: Launched with one service at 11:00 a.m.*
- *1999: Added a 9:30 a.m. service and moved to another school late in the year.*
- *2000: Added a Saturday night service at 6:00 p.m. and took away the Saturday night service for the summer.*
- *2001: Moved to new facility, and added back Saturday 6:00 p.m. service.*
- *2002: Added a second Saturday night 6:00 p.m. service and new 7:30 p.m. service.*
- *2003: Moved Saturdays up an hour to 5:00 and 6:30 p.m.*
- *2004: Added an 8:30 a.m. service on Sunday and went to 8:30, 10:00, and 11:30 a.m.*

- *2004: Added 8:30 plus a Sunday night video venue 5:00 p.m. and college service 6:30 p.m.*
- *2005: Added another service on Sunday at 1:00 p.m. and cancelled the college service 6:30 p.m.*
- *2005: Plans laid to add back the college service.*
- *2006: Added a second site in Kingsville, Texas.*

Big Churches Were Once Small Churches

Over the last couple of years, Bay Area Fellowship has been featured in *Outreach Magazine* and has had extensive news coverage in the city to the point that leaders from all over the U.S. come to BAF to check out how they've accomplished so much in such a short time with so little in the way of resources. Often they will hear someone say, "Yeah, I'd have 4,000 people too if I had a sound/video system like that." Or, "If I had all this space and these seats, our church could be running 4,000 people too." That's a huge mistake. They forget that just six years earlier BAF started with five people in a cramped living room.

Bay Area didn't have all of this equipment and space seven years ago. They started with nothing but a dream, high standards, and few resources (Bil had secured a salary of $30,000 and personally raised another $50,000). But they believed that God would provide whatever they needed when they needed it. Bil C. knew that what was needed most was a big dream.

BAF registers their people's commitments to Christ through the following means:
1. The registration cards that are dropped in the offering plate
2. Decisions made known in membership class
3. Reports to home team leaders

> ### 4. Conversations with ministry leaders
>
> The names are then put into the master salvation list for the year. Those who have made a decision receive a congratulatory letter with some "next steps" suggestions. Then BAF tries to quickly get these folks involved in a home team, or a ministry.
>
> Because BAF is in a predominantly Roman Catholic area, baptism is handled with kid gloves. Still, roughly 40 percent of those who make a commitment to Christ are baptized when they register that decision. An estimated 30 percent more are baptized over the next few years.

Don't fall victim to the small-church syndrome and feel that just because you're small you can't aim for quality and excellence. You can, and should! It's God's church and so trust God to provide your every need.

So, grasp this picture right now. Your church can be huge just like a giant oak tree. What you have to understand right now is that at the moment it's a small seed inside your heart. What you have to do is allow it to grow by giving it the right environment. We're going to talk a lot about growing that seed throughout the book. Just remember, if you're called, the seed of a great dream is already there.

Not long ago, Bil C. and Ed Young, pastor of Fellowship in Dallas, Texas, were having a conversation. "Man, you've been busy. I can't imagine your schedule. It's just got to be crazy," Bil C. said. Ed replied, "Bil, I do the same thing you do." "No, you don't," Bil C. replied. "You're Ed Young!" Ed just looked at Bil and he said, "Bil, I'm just a pastor, man. I've got to write a sermon just like you do, raise my kids, and go to staff meetings." And then he said something that made Bil stop in his tracks. He said, "The only difference between me and you is that I have the same problems, I just have more zeros on them."

Think about it. The only difference between a huge church and a small church is the number of zeros. The BAF of today is not much different than the BAF of six years ago. There are just a few more zeros.

Still, people will say, "Well, but you've got all these children's workers and we can't get three." We know. Bil C. remembers when they only needed three for the whole weekend, and then they only needed thirty, and now they need a hundred and thirty! The same is true with money. BAF is still strapped for cash. The offering is still barely enough to be able to pull off what they need to do. That's normal. That doesn't change as a church gets larger. The only thing that changes is the number of zeros.

So don't let size or lack of funds squelch your dream. Instead we want you to dream BIG. You'll always have troubles. They'll never go away. They just have more zeros by them.

But you know what? You cannot become all that God wants you to be unless you have those problems. That's what makes you into the person God intends for you to become. You see, we ask God to grow us into great leaders, but then ask for God to remove the very struggles that will grow us into great leaders. Big dreams will plow right through the struggles.

Remember, as you read through our book, seven years ago this church was nothing more than a dream. Today it is the home to over 4,000 people who worship each Sunday, with over 100 people committing their lives to Christ a month. It can happen in your church too.

Focus Time

- •What was the last big dream you had? Was it big enough for only God to accomplish? If not, what will it take for you to dream bigger?
- •What feelings emerged as you read the story of Bay Area Fellowship?

CHAPTER TWO

A WILD AND CRAZY GOD

Our prayer is that this book will be a turning point in your life and in the history of your church. We hope God will get a hold of you in such a way that you will dream bigger dreams and you will take bigger faith risks and you will step out for God more than you ever have before. So get ready to be challenged to do things you never dreamed you could do. Let God pull you out of your comfort zone and say, "Let's grow, let's do some things we never dreamed we would do." When you follow Christ, he will lead you to a life that challenges the status quo.

Fast Growth Is Biblical and God Expects It Today

Acts 1 and 2 tell us that the early church went from 120 believers to 3,120 believers overnight. But that's not all. Acts 2:47 tells us that "each day the Lord added to their group those who were being saved." The number of Christians was growing daily! Acts 4:4 says that many of the people who heard their message believed it, and the number of believers totaled about 5,000 men, not counting women and children. So, how many people are we actually talking about here? Conservative estimates at this point put the number of believers around 20,000. In the first year after Christ's death, the number of believers went from 120 to 20,000.

Not only is crazy, go-BIG, huge growth possible, it's biblical and God wants it!

God wants his church to grow because as it grows, so grows the kingdom.

That's the blueprint God gave us. We need to get out of the mind-set that looks suspiciously on churches with large numbers of people. We need to realize that biblical growth has nothing to do with being small.

What's keeping you from asking God to multiply your ministry? Right now, would you just ask God to unleash the dream you have? Would you ask God to help you reach the entire city?

What do you think God is going to say? "No, I don't want to do that"? God wants to do just that. So what's holding God back if we know it's biblical; if we know it's the blueprint that God gives us? We are! But God is just getting warmed up. Acts 5:28 tells us "You have filled all Jerusalem with your teaching about Jesus." Acts 6:1 says "The believers rapidly multiplied." It is only now that they use the word *rapidly*. So from 0 to 20,000 Luke didn't use the word *rapidly*. Luke says that now that they are warmed up they're really going to start growing. This is crazy, psycho growth. It just went nuts like a wildfire. And that's what God wants to do in your ministry.

God Wants Your Church to Reach the Tipping Point

This wildfire of growth was not over. Acts 21 uses another word in regard to the growth—*myriads*. That means tens of thousands of believers now in Jerusalem. The number of believers at this point in the story is staggering. Especially when you realize that Jerusalem had only around 55,000 inhabitants at the time. The church in Jerusalem passed within their city and region what Malcolm Gladwell calls the "tipping point." [1] The tipping point occurs when you're pouring a big bucket of water and get to the point where it all gushes out of the bucket seemingly at once.

The time will come for a tipping point in your ministry. That's the kind of growth God wants to give your ministry. It's the heart of God; it's written all through God's word that God wants your church to grow.

Some people might be impressed by Bay Area Fellowship's growth in the last two to three years. But Bil C. isn't. He calls what's happened "stupid growth":

> We just show up and it grows. It's not impressive. Neither is going from 4,000 to 7,000 in the next couple years. You know why? Because it didn't take anything strategic to do that, other than space considerations. Strategic growth is when you're running thirty people and asking God to make you into a church of thousands. Strategic church growth is when you say, "Okay God, we have to put the blueprint in place for this thing to go crazy." Right now it doesn't take a lot of strategy; at this point all it takes is more services and more seats. What was difficult was getting our people to understand that they're missionaries in this city and their job is to go reach the people and to continuously put the word out again and again and again and when you put the word out enough, eventually you have an evangelistic explosive tipping point, to where all of a sudden it just goes crazy.

Don't overestimate what you can do in a year or underestimate what you can do in ten or twenty or thirty or forty years. You will hit a tipping point where everyone in your community will know that's the church to attend.

Hitting the tipping point requires years of faithfulness. An overnight success is still about ten years. It takes time, energy, sweat, tears; it is hard work. Don't let anyone tell you that church growth is easy; it's not. Sure, you have to trust God, but you also have to work hard.

The Lead Pastor Is the Stopping Point or the Catalyst

Lead pastor, if your church is not growing, you are the stopping point. If your church is growing, you are the catalyst. It's that simple.

God works through the leaders he raises up rather than through committees.

When God wants to change the world he raises up leaders. God does not change the world by committee. When God wanted to lead the people of Israel into freedom he raised up a leader. When God wanted to help a blind man see again he brought a leader. When God wanted to change people's hearts and lives in Jerusalem, he raised up leaders. When God wanted to change the world in Antioch, he raised up leaders. When God wanted to change the city in Ephesus, he raised up leaders. God works though leaders, not committees.

When God wanted to change your part of the world, he placed you there for such a time as this. We hate to tell you this, but you're it. Start taking responsibility for what God wants you to do with your life.

Every church eventually is a shadow of its leader.

So instead of saying, "Well, if I were in a bigger city," or "If we had more money," or "If I didn't have this bozo on my church board," or "If I could get people to show up," or "If I didn't have this going on," or "If I could just get the right music person." Get over it. Quit making excuses and start being the leader God called you to be!

Leadership is the answer to any problem you have. That's why you're reading this—you want some direction.

So, it's time to take your church and your ministry to the next level. Your church is not going to go to the next level until you do. So you have to be willing to go there. You have to be willing to say, "I want to learn what I need to learn; I want to begin to do this." Ephesians 5:17 says, "Don't act thoughtlessly, but try to understand what the Lord wants you to do." Mark 9:23 says, *"Anything is possible if a person believes"* (emphasis added). Read that one again out loud. Anything is possible. Do you believe that? Then act upon it.

What is your dream, what do you want to accomplish in your church? It's possible; there's no lid on the possibility of your ministry. The only lid on your ministry is what you choose to put on it.

Acts 15:26 says, "[They] risked their lives for the sake of our Lord Jesus Christ." The reason the early church had such extreme growth and radically changed lives was because the people literally put their lives on the line for God's work to happen. Are you willing to put your reputation on the line for your church? Are you willing to try new things that you know your denomination's not going to be happy with?

Which God are you going to serve? Are you willing to follow God's call even if it violates the direction your denomination is going? Are you willing to put your checkbook on the line? Are you willing to spend more money than you think the church can bring in? Or are you going to let the checkbook be the God in your life? Are you going to let the facility be the God in your life? What is going to be the God of your life?

We want you to do something right now. Look at Acts 20:24. Paul said he only wanted to complete his mission and finish the work that the Lord Jesus gave him to do. He said he just wanted to complete what God first gave him to do. He had to remember what God first told him to do and never let that go away. What has God called you to do? Do you still get goose bumps when you revisit your call? Are you living up to it? If not, now is the time to step forward and say, "I will be what God called me to be." [2]

Things Start Happening When You Start Praying BIG

You have to start praying crazy big prayers like, "God, help us do more than we've ever done before. God, would you just double our church in the next year? God, help me begin to see our church twice the size it is today. Help me see our church four times the size it is today. Help us start acting like a church twice the size it is today so that one day we become that church. God help us bring Christ to our entire city!"

How does a pastor act in a church with a thousand people? Go visit one and begin to act that way; do the things they do and you'll have a church of a thousand one day. That's how it works. You begin to do those things and put those habits in place and God will grow your ministry to the expectation level you have.

Your church is doing exactly what you expect it to do. Ephesians 3:20-21 says, "Now glory be to God! By his mighty power at work within us he is able to accomplish infinitely more than we would ever dare to ask or hope. May he be given glory forever and ever through endless ages." May God be glorified for the vision you have.

Is your vision so impressive that it demands the glory of God? Is the very thing that you're attempting so crazy that God has to bail you out? Are you stepping out on faith to the point where you say, "I'm having to put my church on the line to do this. Some people might get mad at me. What if they don't like this?"

Listen carefully: if you need "them" to like you, you can't lead them. If you need "them" to like you, you can't lead. You can't need the church or its approval and lead. You've got to go beyond that and say, "You know what, it is not about me working for the church. I serve God in the midst of the church and they work for God. It's all about the glory of God." This is not to say that you are not called to be a team player. You are, but pastor, you are called to lead the team! A great team always has a great leader.

We've got to keep the vision thing a God thing and not a people thing. Leaders should never ask their church what it wants to do. What matters is not what we want but what does God want for your church. What does God think you can do? It doesn't matter what "they" think is realistic. What does God want to do?

God's economy is different than ours. We should ask, "What's possible under his leadership?" Leadership is not based on who we think we are or what we think we can accomplish. It's about humbly going to God and saying, "God, I need you, I desperately need you, or I will screw this up." And when God clearly reveals his vision and you do the steps that he's told you to do, amazing things happen.

A Church Never Outgrows the Vision of the Pastor

The church will never outgrow your vision. So, if you want a bigger church you better get a bigger vision of what God wants to do through you.

God never gives us small dreams. If your dream doesn't scare you a bit, it's not from God.

Some of you need to change your vision of your leadership style. "Well, I'm just a small-town pastor." Yeah, okay, so was Spurgeon, that's fine, so was the Apostle Paul. Gideon was from a small town, he didn't have much going for him; he just wound up leading the nation of Israel, not to mention the fact that Jesus was from Bethlehem. Can anything good come from Bethlehem?

It's not about where you're from, or what education you have, or whether you're the right skin color or have the right pedigree. None of that matters in God's economy. God wants you to get over yourself and realize it doesn't matter whether you think you've got it or not.

Neither of us was ready to be the pastor of the size church God called us to lead. So God had to get us ready by growing the church, and growing us as the churches grew. So now we've got to be ready to grow and learn. Most of the time we still feel very ill-prepared. Many times Bil C. walks onto the stage of BAF, or Bill E. speaks to a room full of people he's never met, knowing that they are really going to have to rely on God to make it through that moment.

God prepares us for leadership by growing the church and watching us catch up.

We both make mistakes; just ask our staff. You're going to make mistakes too; but you can't worry about that stuff. You've just got to step out there and do it anyway, just keep trying and keep doing things because you know what? You're going to make mistakes, but you're going to do one thing right, and because of that one right thing, God grows the church. You can't let that failure stuff hold you back. God knows our tendencies so he give us this verse: "Fearing people is a dangerous trap, but to trust the LORD means safety" (Proverbs 29:25). So, you're ready to act on the vision God has given you. Cast it. Cast it everywhere you go. But remember— managing the vision is much harder than casting a vision:

13

- Does your vision include making disciples? If not, it's probably not from God.
- How often do you cast the vision? Remember how often Nehemiah reminded the people why they were building the wall.
- How many other leaders are casting the vision with you?
- What do you have in place to ensure that the vision is cast on a daily basis?
- Do you spend the majority of your time on the issues surrounding managing the vision and ensuring that the vision manages you and the church?
- Is every leader in the church focused on ensuring that the vision is being managed?

Do Not Give In to the Fear of Failure

How many of us, if we're honest, would say, "There are so many things I want to do and I just haven't stepped out because I'm scared. I'm just scared it won't work. What if it doesn't work? What if I'm out of a job? What if I use all the resources to reach out to people and I don't have anything left to pay my bills?" Well, God's going to have to take care of you then. That's going to be tough isn't it? You'll just have to rely on God.

Do you know how many times neither of us was paid each month in the early years? We can't count the number of times. But you know what always happened? Eventually the money came in and we could still take care of our families.

We know this is a difficult issue. Often our wives would get nervous. "What if the money's not there? We've got kids." But you know what? We can always sell used cars and make a living. So let's quit worrying about whether we're going to lose and start focusing on how God's going to win. Matthew 9:29 says, "According to your faith will it be done to you" (NIV). It's based on your faith, it really is.

Your Problem Is Your Promotion

What in your life causes you to say, "If I could only get over this?" Focus on that one thing for a moment. That very thing is not only the stumbling block in your way it can also be your leaping point. The very thing that was meant to block you, can actually promote you. Let us explain.

Being scared to ask for money is no excuse. Get over it!

Bil C. was scared to death to talk about money for a long time. He was always trying to find ways to keep things cheap and relatively inexpensive so building campaigns weren't necessary. He wanted to be the only pastor in the world who figured out how to never have a giving campaign. But he finally realized that very thing was limiting his leadership. In the midst of fear, God used Bil C. in a miraculous way to raise money when Bil faced his fear—more on this later.

When Bill E. left the pastorate to begin consulting he was so scared to get on an airplane that he had to take tranquilizers. To deal with his fear, he took flying lessons and became a certified pilot and now has flown over 3 million miles.

Why did we do whatever it took to overcome our fear? Because the mission is more important than any fear we might have. Every leader is afraid of something (or someone) and that something is usually the limitation to his or her leadership so he or she does whatever it takes to overcome it. What's standing in your way?

Just being afraid doesn't mean you can't lead. Look at it this way—living a life with no fear means you never take a risk. That's not what God wants for you. You need to step out in faith and believe God for bigger things. Remember, "Perfect love drives out fear" (1 John 4:18 NIV).

One of the most frustrating things about being a pastor of a growing church is that the tools you have to learn to grow the church to one level won't work at the next level. As soon as you go to the next level, God asks you to turn in those tools and learn some new ones. You just got good using those tools and now they don't work anymore. Now you have to pick up new tools that are uncomfortable to you.

Don't be afraid to learn a whole new way of leading. To this day both of us still have to pick up new tools and develop new skills. We will talk about some of these changes in pastoral styles and skills in the chapter on breaking barriers.

Pastor, what's keeping you from dreaming?

Commitment Time

It's commitment time. Will you commit to God to dream and do whatever God wants you to do even if it seems crazy? Pray, "God, I'm going to do this! I've been talking about it long enough; I'm going to do it because people need you. God, I will give you my all; I will step out in faith and believe you for bigger things. Please God, allow my church to grow by your pace and for your plans. And God, I refuse to believe that I can be stopped. I know with only you, I already have a majority. Give me boldness; may I achieve the dreams that you have. Please God, make it my promotion today. In your name I pray. Amen."

If you earnestly pray this prayer, God will throw every resource he has at you. He will give you everything you ever need and more, if you will just make it about his kingdom and not about you.

Focus Time

- *What's keeping you from asking God to multiply your ministry? Take time now to pray for God to open your heart for your city.*
- *What one thing is standing in your way?*
- *Do you really, really believe that God wants your ministry to grow, and that if it isn't, you are the problem?*
- *When was the last time you encouraged your people to invite their networks of people to worship with them?*

- *Are you willing to go to the next level of leadership? If so, have you figured out yet what would that take?*
- *What things are still getting in the way of you stepping out on faith to accomplish the impossible for God?*
- *Are you allowing the lack of money to stand in the way of your BIG dream?*
- *Take time now to pray the prayer in the Commitment Time conclusion.*

CHAPTER THREE

STRUCTURING YOUR CHURCH FOR GROWTH

Three forms of church governance dominate the church landscape today: Congregational, in which the congregation gathers to vote on all mission, administrative, and management issues; Representative Democracy, in which a group of nominated and elected members gather to vote on important mission, administrative, and management issues; and Apostolic or Pastor Led, in which the pastor makes most of the strategic mission decisions and delegates the administrative and management decisions.

Feelings usually run high as to which one of these forms of governance is the best. However, by far, most of the churches using congregational or representative democracy are leftovers from modernity and are either dying or on a plateau. On the other hand, the vast majority of thriving churches today are Apostolic or Pastor Led. Even in those churches that boast of team-based leadership structures, when it comes to a deadlock on a major issue among the staff team, the lead pastor makes the decision.

We also noted that the thriving churches using Congregational and Representative forms of governance have figured out how to circumvent as much of their governance systems as possible.

Bil C. functions in an Apostolic form of church government and is able to lead assisted by the church structure. Bill E. functioned in a Representative Democracy form of church government and spent an inordinate amount of time figuring out ways to lead authentically and effectively when structure actually hindered most forms of biblical leadership. One of the results in the difference is that Bil C.'s church reached more people for Christ. This ratio is true everywhere—Pastor Led churches reach the most people for Christ, period!

We know it is impossible to reconstruct one biblical structure from the Scriptures. Too many words like *elder, overseer, pastor,* and *shepherd* are used interchangeably (Acts 20). However, we do think there are some structural principles in the Scriptures that should be recognized and applied to today's church. Let's look at them.

Democracy Is Great for a Nation but Not for a Church

Many thriving churches today have some form of Apostolic or Pastor Led governance (from now on we will use Pastor Led when referring to this form of governance). By *Pastor Led* we mean that the lead pastor is free to make all mission decisions unencumbered by as few checks and balances as possible. More on this in a moment.

Don't feel as if you must apologize if you are a Pastor Led congregation because neither Congregational nor Representative Democracy are biblical.

Many traditions feel as if such a structure is at best unwise, and at worst unjust. Most traditions prefer some form of democratic government and place more emphasis on a balance of power than the ability of the lead pastor to lead. In these churches, the laity does most of the administration and the paid staff does most of the ministry. We feel it should be the other way around. The problem is that neither congregational nor representative democracy is biblical.

If the will of God was always conveyed through individuals in the Scriptures, what gives us the right to think it can be conveyed today through a committee or board?

Instead, God works this way: God calls a person to lead and gives that person a vision. That leader then shares with the congregation what God's plan is for them. If the leader messes up, God and the board hold that leader accountable and the church usually gets another pastor.

The rule of thumb we see working in the thriving churches today is *the less democracy in the church, the more authentic and effective the church can be in advancing the kingdom of God!*

We know this runs counter to much of what you read today. All we ask is that you examine the Scriptures and the churches that are having explosive growth. What you will find is that the Bible is void of any reference to Representative Democracy or Congregational rule and the pastors of these thriving churches are hamstrung by boards or committees that micromanage the day-to-day ministries of the church.

So why then do most denominations require democratic rule?

We can think of two reasons. The most obvious reason is a fear of one person becoming a dictator. And we agree that dictators are not what God intended. But, we find it sad that some people invariably attach negative behavior to biblical forms of leadership.

The second reason, which is more subtle, is that some people have sold out to the culture of our times. Even though democracy isn't found anywhere in the Scriptures and all of our denominations are the result of the actions of one person, and not a group, they choose a human model (democracy) over a biblically affirmed model (Pastor Led).

Now, here is the best part. The very people who rant against referring to the pastor as C.E.O. require that same pastor to function in a corporation style of church complete with checks and balances. It doesn't make sense unless we are afraid of having strong leaders who listen and act on God's leading.

We give our president power to send our troops into battle because we understand the importance of leadership in wartime. Well, folks, wake up! God's people are engaged in the most important battle in the history of humankind—the battle for the salvation of the world. That battle requires leaders who can lead without numerous checks and balances.

We teach our children about the leadership of David, Jesus,

Paul, Priscilla, Lydia, Peter, and even the founders of our denominations, all of whom lead from personal spiritual authority. And yet, we deny that very form of leadership to our leaders today. It doesn't make sense.

Perhaps the issue is how people view the meaning of spiritual leadership. Perhaps all they mean by it is being a role model to others without requiring action. But that is not the kind of spiritual leadership we see in the Scriptures. Leaders in the Bible not only lead by example, but also by giving directions to the church on what it should be and do, and then holding it accountable.

Pastor, if you don't lead, someone else will no matter what your formal structure says. Some group or person always steps up to fill a leadership vacuum with negativity.

So pastor, don't feel afraid to lead. And lay leader, don't be afraid to let your lead pastor lead. That's the way God intended it to be.

Again, we can hear your concerns. *But what about the abuse of power? Who holds the pastor accountable?* We admit, some leaders will abuse power; no question about it. But why build a structure around something bad that could happen? Why not build a structure around trust that can result in good things happening? *Let your pastor lead and see what God can do!*

Pastor Led Churches

Over the past two decades we have noticed two phenomena taking center stage in church leadership, both of which mirror a willingness to embrace strong, pastoral leadership at the helm, even in a team-based environment. Either large congregations are emerging with a strong central figure at the helm, or young pastors are avoiding the denominational route and heading off on their own to start congregations that they think have a more biblical feel to them than even the best established church. In both cases these congregations are clearly Pastor Led.

And, one quality stands out above all the rest in every one of these pastors; *they pastor as spiritual leaders who listen to God rather than corporate leaders who lead based on democratic rule.* Even if these pastors function in a denomination that requires democratic rule, they find ways to get around or minimize the effects of democratic rule and provide biblical leadership.

Some Details on Leading

Don't think we are encouraging lead pastors to become micromanagers. We are not. By Pastor Led we mean the lead pastor must have total responsibility for making the big strategic, mission decisions. The lead pastor delegates; administrative and management decisions are delegated across the organization to both paid and unpaid staff. Some examples might help:

- The lead pastor should make all the decisions about hiring senior staff and delegate that power to other staff to hire and fire those they supervise and work alongside. In a small church, gaining the right to hire and fire is one of the most important steps a pastor can take toward actually being able to lead effectively.
- In the smaller church the lead pastor is responsible for selecting the lay leaders of the core lay teams that are led by paid staff in larger churches.
- The lead pastor hires and supervises an executive pastor and turns over all of the hiring and firing of the senior staff to that person.
- The lead pastor or executive pastor hires a business manager and the business manager hires, supervises, and fires his or her team.
- The lead pastor decides the church will become a church *of* small groups but leaves the details to the person in charge of small groups.
- The lead pastor is responsible for making recommendations on major budget decisions.
- The lead pastor decides when, how, and where to do an existing or new worship service, but delegates the logistics of the service to other staff.
- The board holds the lead pastor accountable to the DNA of the church but does not meddle in the mission decisions of the lead pastor. If the board does not like the direction the church is going, the board can fire the lead pastor.
- The board, chosen by the lead pastor and not nominated and

elected, partners with the lead pastor in making policy decisions. Together, they set executive limitations such as: "The lead pastor cannot make unilateral mission decisions that go beyond the agreed upon financial resources of the church." Or, "The lead pastor cannot do anything or make any decisions that violate the agreed upon DNA of the church."

- The lead pastor should delegate all clerical, maintenance, and most management issues.

In most dying churches we have seen run Congregational or Representative Democracy, the hiring and firing of senior staff is seldom the sole authority of the lead pastor. Even if the lead pastor plays a major part in the process, a committee on personnel still has the final say. In many of these churches the lead pastor has little or no say in this matter. Even decisions regarding the worship service are often made by a lay committee with little or no input from the lead pastor. We think such decision making is not only unwise, but violates New Testament principles.

Even though Bil C. works in a Pastor Led structure, he functions as in a team-based environment. He constantly is exploring new ideas and possibilities with his staff and key leaders. But when the final decision is made, he makes it. Every study we have seen suggests that teams seldom if ever outgrow their leader. Take a great leader away from a great team and the team becomes mediocre and vice versa. Every great team requires a great leader and every great leader requires a great team. [1]

The Pastors Are the Elders

In the early years of Christianity the leaders of a congregation were called *elders* or *overseers*. Their primary role was to manage and shepherd the body—no committee or board was involved. They accomplished leadership in teams of highly qualified individuals, with one of the elders serving as the primary leader (Acts 11:30). The number of elders was normally kept to a small number. The same is true today in our largest churches. Willow Creek has only six elders and Fellowship Church in Grapevine has only three (at the time of this writing).

So the Scriptures as well as documented research of effectiveness in carrying out the Great Commission are clearly in favor of Pastor Led congregations. Both of us fail to see why most congregations choose the democratic style of governance.

A closer reading of the New Testament writings reveals six specific functions of elders managing and shepherding:

- Teaching the word of God and maintaining doctrinal purity (Acts 11:23; 20:30-31)
- Modeling Christ before the church (1 Thessalonians 2:10)
- Disciplining the controllers (1 Corinthians 4:14)
- Overseeing financial matters (Acts 11:20)
- Praying for those who are ill (James 5:13-16)

All of these are based on a Pastor Led form of leadership.

Protected and Held Accountable

What we find in most of the great thriving churches is a leader who is both protected and held accountable by the structure. These churches know that the vision is not nearly as important as the visionary. Anyone can have a vision. The important thing is, is that visionary protected legally, spiritually, emotionally, and socially, so he or she can get his or her job done? We've got to learn how to protect our church leadership.

PROTECTION — **PASTOR** — ACCOUNTABILITY

The pastor stands between protection to lead and a firm method of accountability so that the pastor is free to lead but is held accountable when he or she leads outside the agreed upon boundaries.

Protecting the leader begins with having a biblical structure that allows the pastor to have the freedom to lead as the spiritual and administrative leader. The more checks and balances a church puts on the leader the less likely the leader can lead, much less lead with innovation.

Due to a nonbiblical structure, most church leaders spend inordinate amounts of time trying to get board members, who have turned into power brokers, to go along with their new idea. Getting buy-in from the people is essential, but when the power to call the shots is placed in someone's hands other than the lead pastor's, time is wasted. And in a world like ours that is rapidly changing and more and more people are dying without Christ, time is of the essence.

People oftentimes ask us, "How you are held accountable?" Often what they really mean is, "How does your church control you?" Do you see the absurdity of that—wanting to control the spiritual leader of the congregation?

It's little more than a knee-jerk reaction to the abuses of leaders in the past. So in reaction we don't follow the Scriptures and we hand over power to the congregation. We can't hand over power—not if we want to be a kingdom builder.

Be Massively Accountable; Just Don't Give Away Authority

Even though Bill E. led a church with lots of checks and balances, he found a way around the burdensome red tape, and by doing so began a domino effect that resulted in the restructuring of his entire denomination over a ten-year period. However, because he found ways to be the spiritual and administrative leader, he had to handpick a group of people whom he trusted and met with every month for the purpose of accountability.

> *We think it is better to err on the side of giving the leader too much freedom to lead than on the side of having so many checks and balances the leader can't lead.*

Bil C. has an accountability partner who holds him accountable for things from how much time is he spending with his family to how he is handling his and the church's finances. Bil C. also has mentors around the nation that he meets with regularly who have complete freedom to speak into his life, and approach his staff, not to mention his family, with questions on how Bil is doing.

Every pastor needs to be held accountable. But don't be fooled. Accountability doesn't happen by accident. You have to create it. Most pastors don't understand this fact. Accountabilty isn't merely electing or appointing a committee to hold you accountable, as is believed in most denominations. For accountability to be authentic three things must occur:

- Trust has to be present.
- Both parties must agree to enter into the accountability process.
- Those holding you accountable should be at least as committed as you if not more.

> *We found that most truly effective pastors find their primary accountability in other pastors in whom they have placed their trust. Sheep do not discipline shepherds.*

Keep in mind that strong accountability doesn't mean pastors won't fall. Many pastors who have fallen morally have had massive structures of accountability everywhere in their life. We have to choose to follow the accountability. It doesn't just happen. We can put all kinds of safeguards around us, but if we choose to fake people out and lie about things, accountability breaks apart.

Accountability Is a Heart Issue

Accountability has more to do with your heart than with a system of governance. You can legislate morality. In 1 Peter 5:2 pastors are told, "Care for the flock of God entrusted to you. Watch over it willingly, not grudgingly—not for what you will get out of it, but because you are eager to serve God." Clearly that is giving pastors a high degree of accountability. We have seen preachers use the church for personal gain. Clearly the scripture is saying don't do that. Pastors are called to take the high road and live as though they were accountable to God.

Keep the Structure Simple and Small

Although the New Testament does not give us a precise form of church government, it does seem to suggest that we keep the structure small and simple. But over time, church groups have increased the structure to match the corporate world of the time. We don't think that's a good practice. We don't need any more structure than the New Testament suggests. For example, the Scriptures clearly teach that the church is led by Christ and that the functions of the church are led by elders, overseers, pastors, or shepherds (all are used interchangeably). However, only one set of elders is found in the Scriptures, and this is the pastors. If you want to advance the kingdom quickly, you need paid elders.

You will probably need a board to be legal in your state and with your denomination (if you are in one), but all the board needs to do is sign documents and hold the lead pastor accountable. When you find people who run from the spotlight and don't want their name in lights and are on the same journey you are on, put a small handful of them on your church board. According to many church growth experts from Lyle E. Schaller in *The Very Large Church*, to Aubrey Malphurs, *Planting Growing Churches for the Twenty-First Century*, the larger the congregation, the smaller the board needs to be.

Don't feel the pressure to put people on a board because you think you have to have a certain amount of people. Bay Area has three board members for 4,000 people. Keep the decision making in the hands of a few spiritual leaders.

How you relate to your board is important. Spend time with them. Take them to see some of the great churches in the U.S. Let them see firsthand what God is doing in the world. Develop these people into spiritual giants who are on the same journey you are on. Many pastors who have small boards meet with them weekly and treat them as if they were paid staff. [2]

The key to structure is for the pastor to be able to lead and the people to be head-over-heels in hands-on ministry. The following chart shows how the church should function.

Nonbiblical Model	**Biblical Model**
Laity Do Most of the Administration	Staff Leads Most of the Administration
Staff Doing Most of the Ministry	Laity Doing Most of the Ministry

In most dying or plateauing congregations the laity make most of the decisions, both missional and tactical. We don't think that is the way God intended for the church to function. Instead, from the Scriptures it appears that decision making was left to the elders, who were the pastors, and that most of the ministry was accomplished by those who were not elders. We even don't like having to use the words *lay* or *laity* since the way the words are used today is far from the way the New Testament writers meant for them to be used. But in order to communicate we see no other words to use.

Trust Is the Issue

Any form of biblical Christian governance has to begin with strong leadership and trust. First Peter 5 admonishes the pastor to care for the flock God has entrusted to him or her. Clearly that is laying some accountability on the pastor. You can take care of people and take advantage of them at the same time.

All of us have seen pastors use the church for personal gain. Because of that some people try to make pastors feel as if they are on a power trip if they do not create a leadership team over them. Usually these people are the power-hungry ones and just need to learn to trust the leaders in the church as the Scriptures suggest. If some people don't trust the leadership, they don't need to create a board that monitors them, they need to find a church where they do trust the leadership. We've seen countless times when a church creates a church board to oversee the pastor to make sure foolish decisions are avoided, only to have the church board make decisions that cause the church to begin to decline.

. The reason most people don't trust their pastor is because of something that happened in another church or with another pastor. So you can't expect them to trust you immediately. You can help them work through that if they are willing. If they aren't willing, there are plenty of other churches that would better meet their needs, or yours.

So What's a Person to Do?

So, if you are called to give leadership in a denomination that requires Congregational or Representative Democracy, what are you to do? In no way are we suggesting that you should do something dishonest. But we are suggesting that any structure can be massaged to where it can allow a leader to lead. Look at Bill E.'s ministry.

Bill E. pastored twenty-four years in one church and grew one of the largest congregations in the area during that time, but he spent many hours working on getting the structure to work for, rather than against, ministry. The results of his efforts were an effective church and a change in the entire denominational policy. It's a story that can be quickly told in two acts.

Act one took place when Bill convinced the personnel committee, known as the Staff Parish Relations Committee, to discontinue hiring and firing and holding the entire staff accountable, and only hold him accountable and allow him to hire and fire and hold the rest of the staff accountable. The second act took place years later when the church decided it could no longer follow the denominational guidelines for their size church, which required some 360 people to be on boards and committees. Instead, the church went to one small committee that took care of all of its administrative matters. The result was much more rapid growth. Ten years later the denominational administrative structure recommended for the denomination's churches was radically changed.

So you can function within a structure with checks and balances and find a way to give solid spiritual leadership; it just takes more time and energy away from the advancement of the kingdom. The price is higher than if you had the much simpler Pastor Led structure.

So whatever you do, never be afraid to lead. Never feel as if you have to apologize that you are in charge. When you shy away from leadership you are abdicating the God-given role of an elder. If you don't lead, believe us, someone else will be glad to lead for you.

In the next chapter we turn to a more detailed description of the role of the pastor.

Focus Time

- *What feelings do you have about the discussion of Pastor Led versus Congregational or Representative Democracy?*
- *Do you have an accountability system in place with your peers rather than within your congregation?*
- *If you function with a Congregational or Representative Democracy, have you found ways to make it more effective and allow you to lead? If not, are you willing to try?*
- *Take time to look for ways to streamline your church structure so that most people are in ministry rather than committees.*

CHAPTER FOUR

IT'S TIME TO LEAD, PASTOR!

The role of the lead pastor is the single most important role in the church. It doesn't matter how the church is structured; as goes the pastor so goes the church. We've never seen a church outgrow the vision of its leaders. We're sure exceptions to this statement exist, but to pull one of these exceptions off would be akin to swimming upstream—and neither of us is fond of doing that. You know what happens to salmon.

Pastor, work on the church not in the church.

The Scriptures are extremely clear about the role of the lead pastor. According to Ephesians 4:11-12, the role of the lead pastor is "to equip the saints for the work of ministry" (NRSV). Nothing is said about the pastor taking care of people, going to hospitals, preaching sermons, or sitting on committees. The pastor's role is to equip the church, period. In the case of a large church, the pastor's role is to ensure that the work of equipping the church is accomplished, usually through the staff.

Our goal in this book is to help you advance the kingdom as far as God has prepared you to do so. The more you lead the more you will learn how to lead and the more likely your church will grow.

So let's take a look at some of the things you won't read much about in other books.

Set Your Own Agenda

You heard us right—set your own agenda based on your call from God and not what the church wants. This advice is for the leader of any kind of church, either a church plant or an established church that has been around for a hundred years. Do what God called you to do, not what the church wants you to do. It doesn't make sense for God to give you a call and you set it aside to do what someone else wants you to do. That's the reason pastors wind up bitter and spent.

Follow your call, not the desire of the congregation. If the two don't match, you should move on. If you don't lead out of your calling, you will never achieve what God has placed you here to accomplish. So set the agenda.

Now we know that setting your own agenda flies in the face of what most denominational officials or seminary professors will tell you. That doesn't matter; it's not the way to lead. Listening to that kind of advice is one of the reasons most churches are in serious trouble—they have chameleonlike leaders who become what the church wants them to be, and often blame the pastor for the lack of growth, and then fire the person. [1]

Do the Things You Are Gifted to Do

Don't feel as if you have to be everything for everyone or do everything that needs doing. Instead, work toward doing as little as possible. That's right, as the church becomes larger, the less you do, the faster the church will grow.

Of course, you know there is more to it than that. The key to effective and authentic leadership is to focus only on what God has called you to do. So, make a list of everything that you are currently doing and ask yourself, *What on this list am I called to do and what can I delegate so I don't have to do it?* When your list is down to three or four things that light your fire, focus on them. Hopefully, these three or four things are the large-impact issues that will cause your church to grow, such as casting and managing the vision, equipping the paid staff, preaching, and hiring the right people. Focusing on a few major issues frees you up to lead and gives you time to develop the next tier of leadership in your church. People use people to get tasks done, but God uses tasks to get people done. The more you delegate and empower, the more you develop people.

If you are exercising biblical leadership as a pastor, then you probably aren't doing much of the hospital or shut-in ministry. So you will need to make sure a care system is in place so that everyone receives the kind of loving care they deserve. Acts 6:3 gives us an insight into how to do this ministry. Find some people "who are well respected and are full of the Holy Spirit and wisdom," and give them oversight of the care system.

Don't Waste Time with the Naysayers

It's foolish to waste your time arguing with people who disagree with your ministry philosophy. Lovingly help them find the exit. Here's why: once established, the basic ministry philosophy of the church is nonnegotiable.

Bill E. always taught his staff to listen carefully to everyone once and evaluate their perspective. If it has merit, pass it on. If not, don't listen ever again to the second verse of the same tune. Time's wasting.

When Nehemiah was busy building the wall to keep out the barbarians, a group of people wanted to harm him. So they asked him to come down to where they were. Here is what Nehemiah said in response: "They were scheming to harm me; so I sent messengers to them with this reply: 'I am carrying on a great project and cannot go down. Why should the work stop while I leave it and go down to you?'" (Nehemiah 6:2b-3 NIV).

How great is the work you are doing? Is anything more important than advancing the kingdom of God on earth? Is anything more important than leading people to Christ and seeing people baptized by the dozens every month? We don't think so. That's why you can't waste time dealing with the Naysayers. Move on.

"They" never exist, so don't listen to the Naysayers.

Don't fall victim to the "they" syndrome. When someone says to you, "They are upset about this or that," just know that "they" never exist and that you're speaking with the person who is upset. Let him or her know that "they" don't exist as far as you're concerned.

We will write more on how to handle problem people in a later chapter.

Live an Exemplary Life

Throughout the Scriptures the leaders of the church are admonished to hold each other accountable to a life worthy of Christ. When you think about it, you may be the primary example of Christ the person sitting in the pew, and on the fringe, might know. How you live just might determine how they respond to the gospel. All one has to do is read Romans 12:1, 1 Timothy 3:1-13, and Titus 1:5-9 to see how much emphasis is placed on the purity of the life of the lead pastor.

But when a pastor has a moral failure of any magnitude, it's not just the pastor and his or her family who suffer. The whole church is affected. Nothing destroys the momentum of a church more than for its leader to lead less than an exemplary life.

As your church grows, you will find it more difficult to go anywhere or do anything that isn't in someone's headlights. Everywhere you go someone will recognize you. You will truly begin living in a fishbowl.

One other thing—the danger in having a small core of leaders is a real thing. You can lead people astray much easier than if you have a big board. So, take your personal accountability dead seriously, so that your life, doctrine, family, finances, and ministry stay above reproach. Don't just be careful; be beyond reproach!

Admit Your Mistakes

There will be times when you blow it big. When that happens, admit it openly. One of Bil C.'s glaring, most beautiful, audacious mistakes was when he took his entire congregation of 2,500 people in worship and moved them across town. Bay Area was out of room where they were, so they moved to an auditorium that seated 2,500. The result couldn't have gone worse. The church dropped 200 people a weekend for six weeks straight and the move to the new location cost them over $100,000! The decline was so serious the staff became divided over the issue of staying or moving back to the old site. Finally, Bil said to his staff, "Hey guys, we have to move back. I thought this was God's plan . . . I was wrong." His staff rallied behind him and they appeared on stage in worship; Bil told the congregation, "I thought I heard God on this. I know this has cost us money and people, and I take the blame. I led us here, and I will lead us back." Bil admitted his mistake and received a standing ovation. They moved back and the next weekly attendance figures jumped by 600 people.

> *Nothing is more disarming than a humble spirit. Don't be afraid to make mistakes; be afraid that you might not humbly own up to them.*

Don't be afraid to take risks, and when you blow it—and you will—admit it and move on. Your people will move on also. When you confront your own mistakes, your people will trust you, because everyone is attracted to honesty and humility.

> *Even though moving to the auditorium proved to be a mistake, Bil C. now believes that God was leading them to do it. And many of their people still do. Bil C. tells this story that happened while at the city auditorium. "When I was there I met a guy who showed up because we were close to his house. He said it was too far to be here with us but when we moved there he said he would come and check us out. He fell in love with the church and came back over here with us when we moved back. That is the same guy who committed 1 million dollars to our building campaign. I'm pretty sure God knew what he was doing. But that's the way God works. I would rather be a fool for Christ. I'm alright with that."*

Be Humble and Accountable

The kind of pastoral leadership demonstrated in the Scriptures and encouraged in this book requires an extra dose of humility on the part of the pastor. Otherwise, it is easy to get oneself into serious trouble. That is probably one of the reasons Jesus said to the apostles, "the greatest among you should be like the youngest, and the one who rules like the one who serves" (Luke 22:26 NIV).

It is never good for anyone to be without some form of formal and informal accountability. Formal accountability is where you establish a group in or out of the church to whom you are regularly accountable. Informal accountability is where some personal friend who knows you well is allowed into your private life for the purpose of holding you accountable.

Cast and Manage the Vision

Pastor, you are the one who has to get the vision from God and speak the vision to the people regularly. The "vision thing" cannot be delegated and never comes from a committee. You must also be the primary visionary by correcting and protecting the vision. When someone disagrees with it, you must be the number one defender of the vision. Don't defend yourself; defend your vision and let God defend you.

Most people will tell you that arriving at the vision is the easy part. Continually casting it, managing it, and embedding it in the congregation is the hard part. To do so pastors have to be firm and totally convinced that the vision is from God rather than some idea dreamed up by a committee.

Establish Clear Lines of Authority

Hebrews 13:17 tells us to "obey your spiritual leaders." It is important to note that when a leader is questioned continually, there may be a false premise of authority going on. You may have to ask someone who questions everything a straightforward question like this: "Who do you believe God is calling to lead this church?" If they say anyone other than the lead pastor, you need to, humbly, biblically correct them. One thing that often happens is that some small group, or peer group (informal social circles of people) begins to form what we call a *power group*. These are people who think they need to tell you how to run the church.

Bil C. and an associate pastor of his went to a small group one evening to answer some questions, and found themselves in the middle of a power group. It quickly turned into the Great Inquisition. After answering many questions and being given unsolicited advice on how to lead the church, one question finally brought some clarity to what was really going on. A member of the church asked Bil C., "Who told you guys it was okay to move the church offices? Were you going to check with anyone?" Then Bil said "No, I wasn't going to check with *you*." Then, realizing what was happening, Bil C. humbly explained that he did not need to check with anyone, because God had called him to lead. One man in the group finally spoke up and told the group that they should not be upset, because in the membership class, Bil clearly explained that the pastors are in charge, and then Bil thanked the man (who is a good friend still today) and explained that the group had a false premise of believing they were in charge. Bil C. then explained that by moving the offices the church would save money *and* improve their office situation.

These are just a few situations that may arise in any church wanting to go BIG. The point here is for lead pastors to quit allowing anyone or anything to question their authority, position, or worse yet, calling.

Focus Time

- *Pastor, have we convinced you that it is God's plan for you to lead the church? If so, what do you need to change in the way you lead? If not, why?*
- *Make a list of the things you do well. Are these leadership related? If so, what can you do to spend most of your time on these items?*

- *Who do you spend most of your time with, leaders or Naysayers?*
- *Think about the last big mistake you made. How did you handle it? If you can't remember one, then perhaps you don't take enough risks, because no one is perfect.*
- *Pastor, how much time do you and your staff spend casting, managing, and embedding the vision? Do you spend more time managing and embedding than you do on anything else? If not, you should.*

CHAPTER FIVE

DOUBLE YOUR VISION

Doubling the Size of Your Ministry in One Year

People develop the habits necessary to create the future they want. Another way to put this is, you get what you expect and believe will happen. Most people don't believe what we just said. So they don't try to picture or live into the future. Therefore, they don't have a part in creating the future. But we believe a large part of the future is what we picture it to be. So maybe what you need is a bigger picture of the future.

In this chapter we are going to share with you the secrets we have learned that will help you to double the size of your church. Keep in mind that areas of the country differ and you need to contextualize everything that we will say in this chapter.

The Five Basic Keys to Explosive Growth

We're going to make this so simple it's stupid. If you want explosive growth you have to:

• Lead as if your church is twice its size.
• Ask for explosive growth to happen and position yourself for it to happen.
• Bring in lots of new people from outside your church.

- Retain the lion's share of those new people.
- Equip and motivate the new people to invite their networks.

Now let's explore each one of these steps to doubling the size of your church.

Lead as if Your Church Were Twice Its Size

You need to picture your church as if it is twice the size it is and live into that picture. Doing so will help you get a picture of how to spend your time. You'll realize you can't continue doing some of the things you are doing and personally survive. The questions you need to ask are, *What do I need to stop doing now that I've been doing, and what do I have to begin doing that I haven't been doing?* Once you've made these changes you are well on your way to doubling the size of your church.

Ask for Explosive Growth and Be Prepared for It to Happen

When was the last time you challenged your people to pray for reaching your goal of doubling the number of people finding Christ and worshipping with you every Sunday? Ask them to pray specifically for people they know need God. Say to those who think you are crazy, "You bet I am. I'm crazy about wanting people to find God!"

"Be wise in the way you act toward outsiders; make the most of every opportunity" (Colossians 4:5 NIV).

But here's the rub—you can't ask your people to pray if you are not praying. So again we ask, *When was the last time you prayed for God to double the size of your church?* It is a huge deal, so make it a part of your life.

One night Bil C. asked his people to commit to ten hours of prayer a month. He asked them to put their name on a piece of paper to show that they were committed to prayer. He then told them that while they were praying ten hours during that month, he would pray one hundred hours. Hundreds of people signed up to pray that night. And the church exploded once again. Pastor, you cannot ignore the prayer principle: when you pray diligently, you get big results.

Don't Pray for Rain Without First Getting an Umbrella

Lots of people will pray for God to do something. But how many actually prepare for it to happen? Do you think God is going to answer the prayers of a lazy leader? We can hear God say, "How can I do that when you've not made room for them?"

It's no good to ask God to double your attendance without preparing for the inflow of people. You have to expect it and prepare for it.

> *You have to position yourself to receive from God. If you don't first step out on faith, God won't bless what you're doing!*

We constantly hear pastors say that they need more volunteers and servants but can't find them. If you have a problem finding people who serve, let us ask you a question: if fifty people knocked on your door and said, "I'd love to work in the youth ministry or the children's ministry," would you have anything prepared for them to do right then? Or would you have to respond, "Can I get back to you in a week?" If you're not prepared for people to respond, why are you asking God to provide? You must take those steps of faith by preparing in advance. Don't pray for rain without holding up an umbrella.

Do you want to prepare for God to double the size of your worship attendance? If you do, you must position yourself to receive from God in at least the following ways:

- Space: Do you have enough seating and children's space?
- Parking: Do you have enough parking spaces, and enough time to transition cars on and off your property before the next service begins?

- Servants: Do you have enough servants to keep up with the growth?
- Money: Do you have the money to support the new services, extra support staff needed, and so on?
- Appearance of space: When you walk into your building, does it rival the quality of a mall or other large venue, such as a theatre? Does the atmosphere of your facility send the right message to visitors? Does it say "God is moving today"; or does it say "God moved here fifty years ago"? This does not mean you have to have something new or expensive, but it does mean you need to capitalize on the facility you are using, to make sure it is visitor-friendly, clean, and has good signage.
- Preaching: If your worship services were filled with more non-Christians than Christian, would your preaching need to change? You have to change your preaching style before God will bless you with visitors, and not after, because if you don't you will blow your first impression and visitors will not return. Train your people to appreciate you're designing your sermons for the people who aren't there yet. If you don't design your messages for the people who aren't there yet, those one or two visitors who walk through the door aren't coming back. Are you ready to handle the growth?
- Personal Appearance: The Bible tells us to look at someone's heart, because God knows that his followers have a tendency to look at the outward appearance. Whereas people judge by outward appearance, "the LORD looks at a person's thoughts and intentions"(1 Samuel 16:7). However, if a believer has a tendency to look at someone's outward appearance, how much more will a nonbeliever look at the outward appearance? Does your appearance say nonverbally that you are current, or outdated? This does not mean you should change who you are, but it does mean to stay updated in who you are. If you are a conservative dresser, dress country, or urban, just make sure you match who you are trying to reach, while staying true to who you are. Do you stay current in your speech? I heard a pastor say from the stage one time, "These new fandangled computers . . . I don't know how they work, much less cyberspace." Has anyone used the word *cyber-*

space in the last ten years? He lost the respect and attention of everyone under fifty years old. Leader, remember you don't attract who you want, you attract who you are.

• How are you positioning your personal life, and your family to receive from God? Have you prayed with your spouse and chidren about how a growing church will affect them?

• Keep in mind the importance of balancing between ministry and family, and the only way to balance is to unapologetically put family above the church.

Bring In Lots of New People from Outside Your Church

If you want a full house you need to set a date and invite your entire community to church at the same time. It's one thing to have visitors come in now and then, but we're talking about going BIG and changing a city. That's the whole point of this book. If God is leading you to do something BIG, the way you do that is not by inviting three or four people at a time. Invite thousands of people at one time!

> *"Go out to the roads and country lanes and make them come in, so that my house will be full" (Luke 14:23 NIV).*

Galatians 6:7 tells us, "You will always reap what you sow!" That's a principle that will not be violated. You tell us how many people you invited and we'll tell you how many will show up. If you invite five people, don't expect anyone to show up. But if you invite 150,000 people, you have a chance of filling the place up. So how do you invite that many people at once? Let's count the ways.

Word of Mouth

The number one way to invite people is word of mouth. First of all the cost ratio is phenomenal: zero. The biggest influx of people is when your friends bring their friends, who bring their friends. That's when growth goes crazy. That's why some churches can grow a thousand in worship in one week when it took them years just to get to that same number the first time. The larger the church becomes, the more important word of mouth becomes. We'll say more about this later.

Direct Mail

We both repeatedly used direct mail and highly recommend it. So do many other churches like Fellowship Church in Grapevine, Texas, and Saddleback Church, in Lake Forest, California. In the early years both churches did direct mail many times a year. Direct mail is a very cheap, effective way to tell your story. In some ways it is better than radio or TV. Whatever you spend on that direct mail piece, people at least have to pull it out of their mailbox and throw it away. For half a second they look at it before tossing it away. But they did look. The real power of direct mail is when it's read the third or fourth time.

Advertise in direct proportion to how you want to grow. However fast you want to grow is how much advertising you need to do.

The best time to do direct mail is to announce a sermon series or to invite people to a special event. Bil C.'s church has used direct mail and TV to publicize many of their sermon series. Bill E.'s church sent out three direct mail Christmas cards during December inviting people to one of their Christmas Eve services. The youth spent most of the fall addressing the envelopes by hand. Regular stamps were used instead of bulk mail. Everyone opens and reads Christmas cards in December.

We are aware that not everyone agrees that direct mail is still valid. In some areas it may be overused. But in most parts of the U.S., direct mail has not been creatively overused. We're assuming that a great deal of time has been spent on the copy or that you are using some of the better church advertising groups so that the mailing stands out and is somewhat provocative. We also recommend either mailing a large number, or none at all. Either hit over 50,000 homes at once, or maybe not at all. The only exception to this is if your town is a total of 50,000 homes or less, then you can still have a large impact with mailing to 15,000 homes. [1]

Television and Cable

The larger the church the more important TV advertising becomes if for no other reason than image. Both of us used TV quite frequently. Bill E. found that 2 percent of his church's visitors came as a result of TV ads, and 95 percent of them joined.

We prefer cable over the networks because the declining networks are still expensive. We're talking about thirty-second spots run numerous times during a short period of time. If you have the right person shop for these ads, you're going to get about half of those free. Don't make the mistake of trying to shop for ad placements yourself. You don't know the questions to ask. You need to get someone who works in cable TV to shop the deals for you. [2]

Ad spots on both cable and network TV will vary from locale to locale. So, it's impossible to say how much a church should spend. BAF typically does a series of four weeks and spends $2,500–$5,000 the first week, $1,500 the second week, and $1,000 the third week, then nothing the fourth week. Bill E. was on six times a day for two weeks, then absent for a month.

Whatever you do, don't spread out your advertising. Focus it on a couple of days so that people see so many of your ads that they wonder if you bought the station!

Web Sites

Web sites are mostly for younger Christians who are shopping for a church. Not many non-Christians are going to look at your Web site. But a good Web site can close the deal. So, at the end of each ad BAF always says, "Check us out at www.bayareafellowship.com."

It is now possible for any church to have a professional-looking Web site for very little cost. You can purchase the template and have someone who knows a little bit about Web text and design manage the Web site.

Radio

Radio didn't do much for either of us. When Bill E. used radio he always ran the ads during drive time and used a station that catered to the kind of people he was trying to reach. If you don't do drive time, don't do radio. In some areas radio makes more sense than TV due to the difference in costs per ad. The real benefit of radio is that you are able to target a segment of the population that you can't with TV. For example, radio has not worked well for Bay Area Fellowship, but the student ministry at Bay Area has found radio to be very successful.

Newspaper

Neither of us put much stock in newspaper ads, especially the church page. If you are trying to reach the upper crust of some city, they probably do read the paper. If you must use the newspaper, position your ad in the personal columns, entertainment, or sports section.

Let's Start a Feeding Frenzy by Combining Some of the Above

It's the combination of multiple hits that brings your advertising to a tipping point. Word quickly spreads and becomes a feeding frenzy. We recommend using a combination of word of mouth, direct mail, and cable television.

Here's what we've found to be effective in reaching non-churched people. Put two direct mail pieces in each worship bulletin (always print more direct mail pieces than you need for the actual mailing). At the end of each worship service ask everyone to hold up their two mailers. Then pray this prayer over those mailers—"God, would you lay upon my heart a friend or family member that I can give this mailer in my left hand to." Then say,

"When God gives you a name, write it on the mailer." Then pray again—"God, would you please give us a name of a neighbor or a coworker that we can give this other mailer to in my right hand." Then say, "When God gives you a name write that name on the mailer. God put that person on your heart. And remember, God demands that you do this and reach that person for Christ. This week I commission you in the name of Christ to go and invite them and bring them back."

Take a sharp pencil to your budget and see how much money you are spending on things that have never contributed to the growth of your church. Reallocated, that money might cause a feeding frenzy over your church.

That same week, send out the direct mail piece to as many homes in your area as you can afford. This way the people get the mailer in the mail and also are approached by friends who ask them to come and check out the worship and have the mailer in their hands.

That same week run as many ads on TV as you can afford. Using this strategy means that now they have received the mailer, had a friend invite them, and saw the church on TV. The odds are they are going to check out your church because everywhere they turn they run into your church.

Now we can just hear you saying, "We can't afford to do all of that." Are you sure you can't? Let's look at some options.

Look at your budget. How much of it is wasted on things that have never caused any growth to happen in your church? Why not stop doing those things and divert that money to causing a feeding frenzy around your church? Most churches waste all kinds of money on events and ministries that never result in more people finding Christ. For example, if your budget is under $500,000, you don't need to pay someone to handle the money— let that person go and use that money to take the bushel off of your light. Or, do you have some staff you could do without for a period of time? Most churches have too many support people in the office.

Or, you could borrow the money. Your church has probably borrowed money to build. Isn't the salvation of people more important than buildings? Businesses do it all the time. Is their product more important than yours?

Or, what about savings? We know—you are saving it toward a rainy day; but didn't the ark float by recently? Isn't that money being wasted when it could tell your story to those who need to hear?

If you are really passionate about reaching to tell the story, we bet you can find some place to find the necessary money.

Perception Is Often More Important Than Reality

The first year Bill E. was the restart pastor of the church he stayed at for twenty-four years, he faced a serious challenge. About the only resource at his disposal was a tiny chapel hidden in a wooded section of a growing area. While out in the community, he met an atheist who had a big heart. The man owned a construction firm and had lots of earthmoving equipment. A few days earlier Bill happened to meet and have lunch with the president of a large retail corporation. During the lunch the man told Bill, "You know, every time we remodel a store, our business doubles during the remodeling." The results of these two conversations gave Bill an idea. Why not borrow one of the atheist's bulldozers for a couple of weeks and move dirt around in front of the church?

At the same time, he borrowed enough money to send out 10,000 mailers to the area immediately around the church. The mailers simply said, "Come see what God is doing at Colonial Hills."

After moving the bulldozer around for a couple of weeks, attendance at church jumped from seventeen to ninety. The public perceived that something was happening at this tiny church that was causing it to grow. What perceptions does your community have about your church?

Learn to Focus

The Apostle Paul is famous for saying, "This one thing I do." Most pastors and churches spread everything too thin to make a difference. What you want to do is create big splashes that bring attention to your ministry.

Remember playing tug-of-war as a kid? One of the secrets was learning that you won by getting everyone to pull the hardest at the same time. Focusing on everyone from the front to the back of line all pulling at the same time was the key to winning the tug-of-war. The same is true when it comes to ministry and inviting the public.

Churches talk a lot about evangelism and reaching people but seldom make any big, outlandish push. What you need to do is focus all your efforts on one big, single day—you'll see your church make jumps of 20 to 80 percent on Sunday because you focused everything you were doing on one day.

Retain the Lion's Share of Those New People

In order to retain people today, two things must happen. First, they have to form significant relationships. Second, they need to grow spiritually. Here's how that happened for both of us.

Small Groups that Multiply

Most people think that small groups will help their church grow. That's not usually the case. Small groups help retain the people who are already coming to your church. For that reason you should never focus primarily on small groups and forget your focus on reaching out to the community.

At the same time, any small-group pastor who never talks about multiplication doesn't need to be a small-group pastor. Get as many people as you can into small groups, but keep the focus on multiplication. Never take your focus off winning the world to Christ by inviting new people into your small groups.

Too many churches look at small groups primarily as a place to learn or share. We don't see them that way. We see the goal of small groups to be equipping leaders who will lead other small groups in the future. The growth of people is always the goal.

Small groups primarily do three things: they are the training ground for the future leaders of the church; they are the incubators of faith for the new people coming into the church; and they are the catapults for sending Christians out into the world to invite their friends in to discover the body of Christ.

Call Every Visitor Who Signs In

One of the most incredible learning experiences Bill E. had as a consultant was that the average pastor in a dying church seldom makes personal calls to the few visitors the church has. This fact blows our minds.

Both Bil C. and Bill E. called every visitor who signed in during the early days. Bill E. did it until the church was 500 in worship. Bay Area was over 1,500 in worship before Bil C. turned over the calling of visitors to someone else.

Both Bil C. and Bill E. called every visitor Sunday afternoon. You should also. Every study has shown that people are much more likely to return if they are contacted within forty-eight hours. In Bill E.'s church, laity took a gift to every first-time visitor on their way home from church. [3] It is not unusual in growing churches for first-time visitors to have three or four contacts with the church the first week they sign in.

We know. Some consultants say that it is more impressive for lay people to call. It's just not so. If your church is running less than 500 in worship and your pastor isn't personally calling every visitor, you're making a huge mistake.

Add Another Worship Service

It doesn't matter how many worship services you have, if you are anywhere near 80 percent full in any of the prime hours, it is time to start another service. So you have three services now—add a fourth one. You can find a way to do it if your vision is big enough.

Nothing grows a church as much as adding a quality, indigenous worship service.

The only reason why you can't add another service is because of the limit you have placed on it. Be careful what you allow to come out of your mouth. If you say, "I just don't think we can do that," you probably can't. But if you think you can do it, you probably can. Who would have thought Bay Area Fellowship could run 4,000 in an auditorium that seats only 750.

The History of BAF Adding Worship Services

- •1998: Launch with one service, 11:00 a.m. only.
- •1999: Added a 9:30 service and moved to another school late in the year (18 months in).
- •2000: Added a Saturday night service 6:00 p.m., and Sundays 9:30 and 11:00 a.m. Took away Saturday nights for the summer.
- •2001: Moved to new facility, and added back Saturday 6:00 p.m., Sundays 9:30 and 11:00 a.m.
- •2002: Added a second Saturday night 6:00 and (new) 7:30, plus Sundays 9:30 and 11:00 a.m.
- •2003: Moved Saturdays up an hour to 5:00 and 6:30, and Sundays 9:30 and 11:00 a.m.
- •2004: Added again; Saturday 5:00 and 6:30, Sundays 8:30, 10:00, and 11:30 a.m.
- •2004: Added again Saturday 5:00 and 6:30, Sundays 8:30, 10:00, and 11:30 a.m., plus a Sunday night video venue 5:00 and college service 6:30 p.m.
- •2005: Added again Saturday 5:00 and 6:30, Sundays 8:30, 10:00, and 11:30 a.m., and (new) 1:00 p.m., plus a Sunday night video venue 5:00 and cancelled the college service 6:30 p.m.
- •2005: Plans laid to add back the college service.

Start a new service as soon as you can and then add another service as soon as you can. The first thing Bill E. did when the church jumped to ninety people was to start another worship service. The key is to ensure that you have enough people in that service for it to feel big. Usually this is about 50 percent of the capacity or at least seventy-five people. If you wind up with less than that, say to your people, "Hey folks, there's fifty people here today, which means that you need to go out and bring in another twenty-five people next week. You know you know them." Remember those two mailers in the bulletin? Ask them to take them out and write down a name and then pray the prayer we gave you earlier. If you do that they will bring people. They need to know that you take it seriously.

Equip and Motivate the New People to Invite Their Networks

The key to everything in this chapter is to do everything we recommended in one month. If you do them all in the same month together, you will see explosive growth:

1. Challenge your people to bring someone that week. This is where you give them the direct mail piece or some kind of advertising you've written up and pray over it in worship.

2. Develop a creative sermon series with a high "felt need" appeal. When you put creativity and a high felt need together you get real growth.

3. Send out a direct mail piece on a sermon or series with a real hot topic you know people will want to hear about. Why not begin with a series on "What God Has to Say about Sex"? That will get people's attention, especially if the mailing is provocative.

4. Have the people take the mailers out of their bulletin and pray over the mailers and have everyone give those to a friend. We can't stress that enough.

5. Add another worship service in conjunction with starting your new message series.

6. Build a service based around special days. Special days help

you break growth barriers quickly and enlarge the vision of your people for what they are capable of doing when they work together. A word of warning here. When your church is first starting out, on holidays, everyone goes home to mom. So if you're not a destination church and it's Thanksgiving, your attendance will probably be the smallest attended weekend. You're not yet a destination church. As you get bigger, you become a destination church and people will invite their parents and friends to attend with them to see what God is doing. The best special days are secular holidays, like September 11, Fourth of July, or Super Bowl Sunday, Christmas, and Easter. The special days in the fall are the best because the fall is a great time of growth.

7. Bring in special guests. If you have to spend a lot of money, don't do it. Don't blow your budget on a special guest. It's not worth it. They will not draw that many. They had better be someone who is so incredible that their appearance will cover what you had to pay multiple times over, if you are going to blow your budget. But if you don't have the money, what do you do? What about teacher appreciation day? You know how unappreciated teachers there are. Go out and ask some restaurant to sell you $20 gift certificates for $10 so you can give them to your teachers. Then give them to all teachers who show up that day. What other special days will work in your church without much money? Little League day? Firefighter, police officer day?

It's All Up to You and the Size of Your Vision

Everything in this chapter is doable one way or another in any size church. You just have to be able to visualize your church twice its size and believe that it can happen. So sit down right now and visualize what you would have to do to make that happen. Then go and do it no matter what it costs. Remember, if it's possible you don't need God. If it seems impossible God is probably waiting for you to ask.

Focus Time

- Go off next Saturday and visualize your church twice its size. Write down what it would look like and how it would feel. Get ready to share this vision with your church next week.
- Make a list of the things that you need to quit doing if it were twice its size, as well as the things that you need to start doing if your church was twice its size.
- Develop a sermon series on a hot topic and have a mailer designed to be placed in the bulletin to be prayed over and sent out to the public.
- What sections of your budget could be re-allocated for advertising?
- What would keep your church from borrowing the money for the advertising blitz? What could you do to minimize those issues?
- Don't let a Sunday go by without calling the first-time visitors personally or having someone call if you are over 500 in worship.

CHAPTER SIX

PREPARING TO BREAK
THE GROWTH BARRIERS

W e begin by debunking an age-old question of strong leadership, "Are numbers all you're interested in?" We get asked that question a lot. It bothers us because we know that most people who ask this question usually do so from either a small-church mentality or an inability or lack of desire to grow a church. They don't have a holy passion to transform people and fulfill the Great Commission.

When the institutional churches grow, the kingdom of God grows, no matter how inadequate a church may be. We've never seen a church, no matter how dysfunctional, that didn't have a remnant of true disciples.

It's impossible to disciple all of the people groups of the world without adding numbers to the body of Christ. Numbers *are* people. So if you want to play that game, this chapter isn't for you. But if you have a holy passion to make disciples, read on.

Over the years most effective leaders have learned that several natural barriers stand in the way of continued growth—200, 500, 900, and 1,500 and beyond (all of these are worship numbers, and they are general number ranges, not exact barriers).

Experience shows that each of these barriers has a few secrets to overcoming it. This chapter addresses those secrets.

One of the key roles a lead pastor plays is removing barriers that stand between the church and fulfillment of the Great Commission. One way to do this is through prayer. Another is removing controllers from power. A third is to provide a variety of avenues of service from entry-level ministries to full-time Christian service. A fourth is to take a group of potential leaders under your wing and mentor their character and coach them in building skills for ministry and life. A fifth is refusing to listen to gossip and letting it be known that such activity is not welcome. A sixth is by teaching tithing so that the church is not held hostage to the bottom line. A seventh is to reduce as much of the red tape and committee structure as possible so that new ministries can flourish. An eighth is—we're sure you can add some more ways. The point is, barriers *must* be eliminated for a church to reach its potential.

Keep in mind as you read this chapter that churches typically do not inch by barriers. Barriers are usually broken quickly, caused by something new that has been initiated.[1]

You will notice that the larger the church becomes, the less changes have to be set into motion to break through the barriers.

Issues at Every Barrier

Several issues need attention when breaking any of these natural barriers. Failure to address them makes the barrier that much harder to cross.

You're Not Through 'Til You're Through

Growth barriers aren't as neat as one might think. Churches begin dealing with the barrier long before they get to it and long after they have passed it. For example, the 200 barrier is an obstacle from the moment the church is birthed and is seldom overcome until the church passes through the 500 in worship barrier. In the same way, the mind-set that causes the 500 in worship barrier isn't overcome until the church reaches 700 or 800 in worship. So leaders must begin addressing the next growth barrier as they move through the present growth barrier.

One more thing—as you move through growth barriers, many of the things you had to do to break the previous barrier you still need to do in each succeeding barrier. The only exception is the pastoral style, which usually changes at every barrier.

Leadership Must Grow First

If you yearn for your church to grow to a new attendance level, then you as the leader must grow first. The leadership style that got you where you are will not take you where you want to go. You must begin leading your church like it is already bigger than it is, and then your church will catch up with you.

The opposite is also true. If a church brings in a pastor who only knows how to lead a church smaller than the one called to, the church will eventually shrink to the size the leader knows how to lead in.

Bill E. can remember four transitions in style during his twenty-four year tenure at the same church. Some transitions were more painful than the others, but each one took some training and concentration of effort on his part. The same will probably be true for you. The following chart shows the four changes in Bill E.'s approach to ministry.

RELATIONSHIP BETWEEN STAGES OF A GROWING CHURCH AND LEADERSHIP SKILLS NEEDED	
STAGE OF DEVELOPMENT: AVERAGE WORSHIP SIZE	**LEADERSHIP SKILLS**
0 - 199	CATALYST, PARTNERSHIP, ENTREPENEURIAL, INVOLVED IN EVERYTHING
200 - 499	ONE WHO ANTICIPATES, ADJUSTS TO, AND INTERPRETS CHANGE; WORKS WITH GROUPS, PRIORITIZES
500 - 999	VISIONARY, DECISION MAKER, DELEGATOR, EMPOWERER, EQUIPS STAFF
1,000 +	PREACHER AND STRATEGIST

For a variety of reasons, some pastors simply can't grow a church beyond a certain size. Either they don't want to, aren't willing to pay the price of personal change, or don't have the skill set. In the same way, it is rare for all of the staff at one size church to be able to make the transition to the next barrier. So one of the roles of the lead pastor in moving through barriers is to evaluate which staff is making the adjustments, which staff need retraining, and which staff need to be terminated. As you can well imagine, being willing to terminate staff might be one of the biggest hurdles to crossing barriers ever faced by the lead pastor.

When Bill E. had a staff person who wasn't measuring up to the growth curve, he would talk with the person and let them know they had six months to grow into the present size of the church or he would have to let them go. During those six months he promised the person to provide them all of the resources, training, and evaluation he could to assist them in their personal growth. If they couldn't do the job after six months, he would let them go.

Maximize Your Facilities

Facilities should never dictate how many people you can reach for Christ. Here's a rule that will never fail you—anytime anything begins to approach 80 percent capacity in the prime time, it's time to do something to make more space.

It's hard to grow beyond 80 percent of your space.

If you're out of room, consider the options—relocate, add another worship service, become a multiple-site church, have your people move from one service to another (Rick Warren calls this a "missionary move"), or plant a new church and give some people away. But never allow your facilities to keep you from fulfilling the Great Commission.

Lakewood Church in Houston is a prime example of what can happen when you honor the 80 percent rule. They had been stuck at 6,000 in worship for several years. In 1999 a second service was added and the church doubled to 12,000. Less than two years later they added a third and fourth service and they doubled again to 24,000. Now they are moving into a 16,000-seat auditorium and they expect to double or triple overnight.

In all growth barriers one of the keys is if you don't add space, you're not going to grow. Start with adding services, then when you've maximized your space, hire a good commercial real estate person to help you find another location. Rick Warren's church chose very few of the fifty some sites they used over the years.

Add Staff as You Grow

We've watched numerous churches grow up to 200 in worship without adding any paid staff. Doing so is always a mistake. Next to adding worship services, adding staff who equip people for ministry is a key factor in growth. We're not talking about adding staff who do the ministry. Anyone who is paid needs to be an equipper to be biblical (Ephesians 4:11-12).

In studying many thriving churches we've noticed there is a logical progression in adding staff. The first paid staff person to hire is a worship leader. Failure at this point usually results in a small congregation. If your worship service suffers from bad worship music, it is the worship leader's fault at first. If the pastor does not address it, the fault shifts to the pastor.

Staff who work primarily with people should pay for themselves in the first year or two in two ways: their ministry results in new people; and they equip those people to do ministry and bring in their networks of friends and acquaintances.

After this barrier there is a wide degree of variance in the addition of staff. However, there are four areas of ministry that have to be covered in any size church for it to grow: worship, lay mobilization, administration, and outreach. These may be done by unpaid servants at first, but over time they become paid positions. You may have a great volunteer doing this now, so just bring them on as paid staff and gradually build their work to full-time. If you don't feel they are capable of drawing new people due to a lack of talent, skills, people skills, and so on, don't feel obligated to hire them just because they have been volunteering. Bad volunteers make even worse paid staff.

Never hire a "project" person. That's someone who needs to grow into his or her position. If they will not make an immediate impact to help grow the church, they shouldn't be hired. Never allow a staff member to become *a* mission. By that we mean someone who needs taking care of. Instead, all staff must be *on* a mission.

All staff should pay for themselves in a short time. If they aren't paying their way, fire them, and the sooner the better. Any pastor can hire a staff member, but it takes a leader to fire a staff member. More on hiring and firing in the chapter on staffing.

Dream a Bigger Dream

Growth barriers are usually broken when the pastor dreams a bigger dream. What you must do is visualize a church twice your size and constantly share that vision with your people and work like it all depends on you, praying as you go. If you do, more people come to realize that growth is a core value for God's church. But you must believe that it is God's will for his church to grow. It's amazing what happens when you do.

Develop a Farm System

Leadership development is a key factor at every stage of growth. So it is important from the beginning to set up some kind of farm system for growing leaders.

A farm system is a simple plan for raising up future leaders. You're probably familiar with farm systems in pro baseball. Triple A teams are where the pros scout for their future players. A church is no different. It lives or dies on whether or not it can raise up the number of servants needed to carry out its ministry.

Developing a farm system involves at minimum the following:

- Every person, from junior high on up, is seen as a potential leader.

- The congregation functions as an incubator of faith. The ethos of the congregation is such that people feel encouraged to grow. A conflicted congregation can never develop a farm system.
- A farm system requires systems for identifying, inviting, equipping, discerning, deploying, and coaching leaders.
- Farm systems assume that you mostly hire from within your church. Bil C. has hired 95 percent of his staff from within the church, so they already understand the vision. They already are used to a fast pace, and as Bil puts it, "You don't have to beat out of them the small church mentality that is taught by default at most seminaries."

There are different levels of leadership that you move people through. As people demonstrate a willingness to serve and actually do what they say, they are given more responsibility. The more responsibility, the more accountability and spiritual depth the person must demonstrate. The following rating of leadership has nothing to do with the worth of a person but with the level of his or her responsibility.

- Leader of Leaders of Leaders—The lead pastor
- Leader of Leaders—All staff
- Leaders of Systems—Lay mobilization of small group system
- Leaders of Major Ministries—Small-group system
- Leaders of Programs, short and long term—Sunday school or VBS
- Leaders of Committees—Lowest level of leadership
- Apprentices in Training—Anyone in the congregation
- Visitors

All staff support and work the system. Effective staff regularly raise up new leaders for ministry even if the church has all the volunteers it needs.

Jesus left us the best example of how to develop a farm system. He never invited someone to do a job or perform a task. Instead he invited them to come follow him on a journey. This is key when developing a staff—don't give them a job description; invite them to join you on an incredible journey. Then Jesus spent his entire ministry modeling and embedding his "DNA" (by which we mean values, beliefs, vision, mission) in this small but diverse group of future leaders who decided to take the journey.

Any solid discipleship model has two tracks—modeling and training. The most important is modeling since discipleship can't be taught. Intentional modeling is when all of the leaders, paid and unpaid, understand that their role is to model discipleship to everyone. Leaders are mentors. They make sure there are enough entry-point servant ministries in which people can begin serving alongside their mentor.

People are always asking us, "What is the best curriculum for equipping disciples?" Our response is always the same, "You are the best curriculum."

Don't spend valuable time creating content-oriented discipleship programs that are simply to please high-maintenance believers who think they are mature. Such programs eat up valuable time and money. Maturity is not measured on your words, but your deeds. Maturing Christians don't need another course or Bible study. Instead, they need to apply what they already know. People tend to think of discipleship as going deeper in knowledge. An educator can tell you that the highest form of learning is application, so put them to work serving, the more the better. If the so-called mature are not willing to serve, don't let them mentor anyone else or be in a power position, because you don't want bad DNA embedded into others.

Think about how Jesus did ministry. He did; and the disciples watched. The disciples did; and he watched. Then they did it all. How many entry points do you have for:

- Non-Christians and first-time guests?
- Day-old Christians?
- Maturing Christians?

Watch the Moving Averages

Like the stock market, churches have moving averages when trying to break through barriers. Churches often inch up to a barrier and perhaps break it and then fall back to a lower level. Over a period of years, this yo-yo cycle is repeated many times. If you followed the moving average of the ups and downs, you see the approximate same worship average reoccurring many times. We call that number the *moving average*. We have learned that three things affect the moving average:

1. The coming and going of a new pastor. Either the pastor grows it forward and then leaves or grows it downward and then leaves.
2. The church is over 80 percent capacity in either parking or worship.
3. The mind-set of the congregation simply can't grow beyond that of the smaller reoccurring number.

If you find your church continually reaching a barrier and then falling back, the odds are it is because of one or more of these issues.

On to the Barriers

The next chapter introduces you to the most common growth barriers. Keep in mind that everything in this chapter applies to each growth barrier. Have fun!

Focus Time

•*What kind of a system do you have in place to grow people? If you don't have one, what steps do you need to take to develop one?*
•*As you approach one of these barriers, do you sense a need to grow yourself to another*

level? If so, what do you do to ensure that happens?
- Have you noticed any moving averages over the years? If so, do you think the cause is one of three issues listed above? If not, what can you pinpoint as the reason?
- Make a list of the things you couldn't still do if the church were twice its size. Which of them can you stop doing now without losing your job?

CHAPTER SEVEN

THE GROWTH BARRIERS

The following growth barriers are based on years of research by many people. What we bring to the table is personal experience about breaking these barriers, as well as Bill E.'s experience consulting with over 600 churches. We've both accomplished what we will share with you in this chapter.

The actual numbers may vary from study to study but that doesn't detract from the fact that natural barriers to growth are present in every congregation. Knowing approximately where these barriers begin is important to sustained growth, if for no other reason than the roles played by leadership change at every barrier.

As you read through the barriers, keep in mind that most of the recommendations for each barrier continue over into all of the succeeding barriers.

The 200 Barrier

The 200 barrier is the hardest barrier to overcome. It was by far the hardest level for both Bills to get past. Each barrier after this one got more and more easy. That is why we recommend when planting a church to make sure the second Sunday the attendance is over 200. That way you never have to deal with this barrier.

But if you are already pastor to an established church under 200 in worship, then you must address the following issues.

The Small-Church Syndrome

"Pastor, if we grow anymore, we won't know everyone anymore."

"Pastor, before we go after any more people, shouldn't we take better care of who we have?"

"Pastor, all you seem to care about is the unchurched. Don't you care about us anymore?"

These questions must have been conceived in hell because they betray a basic misunderstanding of what it means to be the people of God and the body of Christ. Everything in the Scriptures suggests that the church was put here to reach people who are not yet Christians—the church was to be salt, light, and leaven to the world.

So, when you hear these kinds of comments it is the duty of the leadership to go on the offense and teach rather than go on the defense. Here's what we mean. Bill E. responds to these questions like this: to the first question he responds, "Isn't it more important that everyone in town know God?" And then he waits for a response. To the second statement he responds, "Don't you realize that our city is filled with people who have never known the love you know? Surely you aren't saying that we should abandon them? Surely you realize that we are nurtured the best as we reach out to others?" To the third question he responds, "Certainly I care about you, but it's time we all grew up in our faith and began doing what God put us here to do—make disciples!"

Bil C. responds to questions like these by smiling back and saying, "That's okay. You weren't supposed to know everyone. That was never a core value of God's church."

> *Knowing everybody is not the definition of a healthy church. In fact, it may be the definition of an unhealthy church.*

Small churches need to know that every large church was once small and that small is never an excuse not to extend the gospel. Give this sentence time to soak in.

The Small-Church Comfort Factor

The easiest size church to manage financially is a church around 150. The church can afford a pastor and a secretary and all is well. Add to that the comfort level in this size church is about as good as it gets. This one pastor can easily be whatever anyone wants him or her to be. Everyone has direct access to the pastor and the pastor can tend to every spiritual hangnail. However, few baptisms occur in this size church. Is it any wonder this is the hardest barrier to cross?

Pastoral Leadership Style

In churches under 200 in worship the church grows by a relational connection to the pastor. Everyone is connected to the pastor and spouse. People come to the church because they love you. That's a nice thing and it makes you feel good and important. But it also causes a problem. They become accustomed to having direct contact with you. As you grow, they can't have such contact and they begin to feel as if you don't care. And if you're not careful, you will fall victim to feeling as if you should try to be everything to everyone and be available to everyone—and that is the beginning of the end. You must realize you aren't their savior and you're not supposed to meet their every need.

> No one grows a church this size by sitting in his or her office or playing on the computer.

To break this barrier the pastor has to begin working with groups and focusing on helping the church continue to reach out. This means that the pastor must spend more time outside the church with the unchurched than inside the church with the members.

The pastor taking care of the membership is the primary reason small churches don't grow. Instead of taking care of the members, the pastor should be growing the members to the point that they realize *the* mission of the church is to introduce people to Jesus Christ.

Most of the Growth Is the Result of the Pastor's Effort

Don't be fooled into believing that people are going to flock to your church just because you're the pastor or because all of your people are inviting their friends. This just doesn't happen at this size, especially if you are an established church.

In a church with under 200 in worship, the pastor single-handedly can bring in enough people to grow it past the 200 barrier.

Sometimes pastors are so busy writing messages that they have no energy or time left to focus on strategic pursuits like adding a service or staff member or advertising or getting out among the public. Instead of spending so much time in the office, we recommend buying another pastor's sermon series, whoever's teaching you happen to like, and teach his or her series for a month. Tell your people what you're doing. In his early years at Bay Area Fellowship, Bil C. used to regularly take other preachers' messages and use them from beginning to end, and give credit at the bottom of his message outlines. This way he could use his time reaching people instead of creating a message from scratch. When you do this, you are freed up to focus on:

- Creating a strategy to draw more people into the doors of the church
- Challenging every individual member to bring someone
- Developing key relationships with potential visitors

Bil C. preached Rick Warren's messages unapologetically for a year. By doing so he could focus on making phone calls (calling every visitor personally every week to invite them back), building relationships with pre-Christians, and raising money to be able to continue doing outreach to help the church grow. (In the dark ages when Bill E. restarted his church, there weren't online sermons like there are today, so he spent less than four hours a week on a message and four days a week reaching out to the unchurched.)

The 200 barrier is surpassed when the leader who was so busy working in the church takes the time to work on the church.

Don't feel bad about using someone else's message. You are trying to go from crawling to walking. You don't need to reinvent the wheel all the time. There's too much good stuff out there to try to come up with everything yourself. A sermon worth preaching once is a sermon worth preaching twice. [1] You'll also become a better teacher this way.

What matters most is that you spend time doing whatever it takes to bring people to worship. You need to be constantly bringing people to your church to move beyond the 200 barrier. You must spend your time with visitors and not with those who are already members. This is painful, but it works.

The 500 Barrier

Breaking this barrier involves leading leaders, and managing servants well, while continuing to reach out. This barrier should be broken as quickly as possible, because this is where church splits often happen. Remember, the small-church syndrome is still with you for some time and if given the chance, most churches will gladly return to the comfort of 150.

Pastoral Leader's Style

As painful as it may sound, at the 500 level the pastor can no longer be personally connected to everyone. Now you must:

- Focus your time on the staff and leaders of leaders. You must lead from in front of the flock instead of alongside it. Most pastors find this phase to be one of the most difficult learning periods of their ministry.
- Think of the big picture and work on results. You no longer have the luxury of being present at every event or being in everyone's home. Now you must remove yourself from the

micro issues of the church and focus on the macro issues that will result in most of the growth of the church.

- Work with groups rather than individuals (except for your staff and leaders of leaders).
- Develop your hiring and coaching skills to the max. Often, this is the straw that breaks the pastor's back. Firing someone you care about is not the easiest thing to do. Yet chances of you having to fire a staff person at this level are unfortunately high because the church has outgrown some staff's ability to help the church grow in this larger arena. Remember, pastor, you cannot afford to ignore a staff member not doing a good job—there are not enough resources to keep an ineffective staff member.
- Spend more time on developing your prayer life. As the church grows numerically, you must grow spiritually. You simply can't give what you don't have. And the larger a church grows, the more it relies on the spiritual growth of its leader.

The time restraints necessary to be able to minister to a group of 400 people will frustrate some of the original members, because they will begin to feel that "you've changed." They aren't invited to dinner/lunch/play golf/visit as much. As you attempt to reach more people than just them, members get offended. They begin to feel as if you have left them behind in your attempts to reach more people. In the case of Pastor Led congregations, when the church is small no one really cares that you make all the major decisions that deal with direction or money, but as the church grows so do the offerings, and some of the original members will begin to feel like the pastor now has too much power.

> *Pastors who are afraid to exercise spiritual and administrative power don't grow churches.*

Pastor, if you're afraid of exercising power you will not get past this level. If you will give up leadership to those who complain the loudest about feeling left out, the lost and unchurched in your community will not get the attention they deserve. You must be loyal to the vision to reach everyone in your community, and challenge your people to get their fellowship needs met in small groups and to serve one another, and humbly ask them to give up time with "their" pastor.

The Role of Staff

When you reach this point, staff becomes as important as the pastor because the lead pastor no longer knows everyone in the church. Now individual staff know people in their respective areas much better than the lead pastor. In essence staff have become the members' real pastor.

So hiring and equipping the right staff becomes one of the most important ministries of the lead pastor. Most often pastors don't have the skills or temperament to hire and fire people. This lack often becomes the primary reason a church doesn't cross this barrier. If you know you lack these skills, talk to someone in your church who works in personnel. Remember, Moses wouldn't have gotten the Hebrews to Canaan without the personnel advice from Jethro (Exodus 18).

Bill E. felt lacking in the area of hiring, but his wife had excellent discernment skills, so he made sure that she had dinner with every major candidate. Other pastors bring an executive pastor on the staff for the purpose of hiring and firing staff. If you don't feel comfortable hiring people, find someone who is good at hiring and let them do it as long as their DNA is the same as yours.

We suggest you hire staff first for loyalty to you as the lead pastor, second for their passion for the mission, and third for talent.

It's never good to allow a committee in the church to do any of the hiring. Wrestling this function away from an existing committee set up by his denomination was one of the first things Bill E. had to do to restart his church. When a committee is involved it always dilutes the cohesiveness of the staff. Either you hire the staff as the lead pastor, or have an executive pastor hire the program staff and a church administrator hire the office and custodial staff.

At this point program and pastoral staff should be specialists rather than generalists. Although they should excel in a particular area, they should be flexible enough to work in other areas as the church grows and its needs change.

Multiplication of Cells and Entry Points

To continue reaching more people you now need to multiply the number of places within your church where people can find a place where everyone knows their name. In the vast majority of cases we've seen, small groups are the answer. But you also need to increase the number of entry points into the church. The larger a church becomes the more people it loses and the more people it needs just to stay even. Often the increased entry points are the committed participants who invite their friends to worship with them.

The 900 Barrier

Few churches grow to this size. Those churches that do grow to this size find the following words to be extremely important:

We can't stress enough the importance of thinking and acting multiplication rather than addition. From now on just adding people won't keep the momentum going.

- Systematic—in the way everything is done. Nothing can be left to chance or shot from the hip. Systems must be in place to close the back door and encourage bonding. Often the most critical issue is finding ways to identify people who are sitting in the seats and have not signaled their presence.
- Multiplication—rather than addition.
- Equipping—rather than delegating and doing programs. Growing people becomes far more important than the type of ministries you have.
- Redundancy—to ensure no one falls through the cracks. It takes more than one safety net to ensure you don't lose lots of people through the cracks.
- Intentionality—to ensure that growth continues. The larger the church becomes the more intentional it must become in following the systems that have been set up to ensure the continued growth of people and the church.
- Accountability—to ensure that everyone has a place where

everyone knows their name. At this size it is easy for things to fall apart simply because no one was keeping track of what is or isn't happening.

• Excellence—because that is what people expect from a large church. At this size people begin to expect far more quality than ever before.

The Large Church Syndrome

At this size the problems are bigger but the solutions are easier and less numerous than in smaller churches.

Four negative things need to be guarded against in large churches:

• People fall easily through the cracks.
• The environment becomes cold and unfriendly.
• The church relies too much on the paid staff.
• The church can quickly fall apart due to financial mismanagement. All of these explain why most of the words above are so important.

Many a pastor has told us that at this level he or she begins to realize that he or she doesn't know all the people in the choir, or all the Sunday school teachers, or all of the small-group leaders. In large churches it is easy for people to attend and never be seen or heard from.

Pastoral Style

At this stage you just don't have time to work with servants. Now you lead and empower the core staff to lead the servants. In doing so, leaders must move from delegation to empowerment. What's the difference? In delegating you are asking people to do something you want them to do or the church needs them to do. To empower people means that you assist them in doing whatever it is that God created and gifted them to do with their lives. Helping people discern their gifts is key to empowerment.

The experience Moses had with Jethro in Exodus 18 is important at this point. The lead pastor doesn't need to ever get bogged down in minor issues. The vast majority of decisions need to be made by someone else on the staff, allowing the lead pastor to concentrate on the major issues.

Not much is written about this level of leadership. That is why you probably need to find a coach. Getting a pastor of one of the larger churches to spend time with you will be difficult but it will be worth the effort. Also, consultant coaches become important. Bill E. is a pastors' coach. Being in some of the largest churches in the U.S. regularly allows Bill to help pastors who cannot get to these larger churches. Bil C. does mentoring for larger churches (400 and beyond) to help them grow, because the fastest way to break a growth barrier is to be mentored by someone who has already done it. [2]

1,500 and Beyond

Whereas multiplying leaders was the biggest challenge at 900, the biggest enemy of the church from now on is pure space. Space refers primarily to acreage, worship space, and parking. Just the sheer magnitude of finding a place for all of these people becomes paramount in the continued growth of the church. The church will need more land, more worship services or more space for worship, and more parking. Failure to multiply any one of these three areas causes the church to lose its growth factor.

For most churches reaching this size, two major space issues emerge—worship and parking. Just consider the following: most growing churches need to provide a parking space for every two people on the property at the peak hours. You can get about 150 cars per acre. If you're running 1,500 in two services, you will need a minimum of three to four acres just in parking. You see our point. Not only does it take more worship services to accommodate the growing number of people, it also takes more acreage for parking. To outgrow parking either stops or slows the growth.

It is not unusual for churches this size to have to do one of the following in order for worship to continue to grow:

- Hold numerous worship services. We need to get over the mentality that we can only do two or three services.
- Totally relocate. This is one of the most expensive ways to solve this space issue. We recommend that you put relocating off as long as you can, and when you do relocate, buy as much acreage as possible. If you are running 900, buy at least thirty acres; if you are running over 1,500 already, buy at least fifty acres. If you cannot afford enough space, then consider multiple locations.
- Develop multiple sites. This is becoming one of the major trends of our time. [3]
- Develop an active parking ministry.

The revolving door is the second biggest enemy of the very large church. The number of people dropping out, dying, or moving is sizable. It is not unusual for a church this size to need to replace 300 to 500 people each year just to remain the same size as the year before. Often no one even knows that the people who have dropped out are gone.

Instead of leaders practicing one-on-one disciple making, they train multiple leaders to make disciples. The goal is not to make disciples but to make disciples who in turn make disciples.

How BAF Broke the 1,500 Barrier

Breaking the 1,500 barrier required a more focused effort on evangelism. BAF had to become intentional with its congregation on the importance of moving service times to make room at the main hours. It also had to take bigger risks as far as subject matter, to draw attention back to visitors coming since its community was getting used to its advertising and programming. BAF also had to make a very big jump into the world of systems. Also, BAF had to build a new layer in staff and move to a management staff that helps steer the ship for the pastor. The

> *senior pastor also had to make personal changes, like slimming his life down, doing less, and improving the quality of the service to a higher level of excellence.*

Multiplication Totally Replaces Addition

Churches that reach 1,500 usually have put into place some form of multiplication system. If they haven't, this is the most critical issue.

We've seen four multiplication ministries used in thriving congregations: meta groups, fractalling, groups of twelve, and permission giving. Let's briefly look at each one.

- **Meta Groups.** [4] Small groups are formed around various forms of affinity. Laity invite friends, relatives, neighbors, and associates into their homes for a weekly time of sharing, praying, and Bible study. This model has four essentials: one, the ultimate goal of each group is to bond and then birth a new group; two, leadership training is at the heart of ministry; three, the pastor must be involved; and four, small groups become the hub of the church.
- **Fractalling.** [5] Fractalling is the constant repetition of something over and over. For our purposes, it is everyone training everyone also to be a leader. Every leader is responsible for four other leaders and their spouses. The four other leaders in turn are responsible for four other leaders and their spouses. So the span of care is limited to ten people. Every leader asks, "Who can I get to help me on this mission?" and, "How can I break this project down into small enough pieces to include lots of people in the mission?"
- **Groups of Twelve.** [6] This model comes out of South America. In this model, all leaders are in two groups all of their lives—a group of twelve and a cell group. The groups of twelve are for those who lead their own cell group and the cell groups are for new converts and young disciples. Each member is encouraged to begin a cell group with his or her converts. The leader disciples them and eventually the group reaches

twelve. The leader continues to reach people, and places them in one of the cell groups under him or her. Each of the group of twelve begin their own Bible study to reach new people for Christ, and to place them in a cell group. The process continues over and over.

- **Permission Giving.** A permission-giving church is one in which people are encouraged to discover and live out their God-given gifts in order to enhance the agreed upon mission of the church without having to ask for permission from a central authority, as long as the person can find two or three people who want to help. Many large traditional churches grow to and beyond this size because they are open to many forms of ministry and allow ministries to bubble up from the laity. These churches have clarity about their DNA, have streamlined their structure to allow ministry to occur quickly, and are very flexible with new ministries as long as they enhance their agreed upon DNA. [7]

Bonding Is Essential

At this level more attention has to be given to people bonding and not falling through the cracks. [8] If you have 1,500 in worship each week, you probably have 2,200 in worship each month. That means you probably have several hundred people no one on your staff knows. These people are likely to become lost in the shuffle if you don't take some positive action. So, if you have not done so yet, small groups need to be formed to provide people a place where everyone knows their name. It is almost impossible to develop a small-group system without a full-time person. This ministry is so important and huge, our next book will be devoted entirely to small-group ministry.

Management Is the Key

Churches that reach 1,500 need to locate the decision making in a small management team. This team is usually less than nine people and includes the lead pastor as either the chair or key member of the group.

Overseeing the spending is often a key issue for the management team since it is easy to shuffle money around from place to place to cover shortfalls. This kind of shuffling of funds represents a good way to get the church in financial trouble, because it fails to find genuine solutions to money issues.

Focus Time

- *How much time do you personally spend bringing people to worship or ensuring that new people are coming to worship?*
- *Has your pastoral style grown to fit the next sized church? If not, what do you need to acknowledge to begin making the changes?*
- *How do you feel about Bil C. using Rick Warren's sermons so he had more time to grow the church?*

CHAPTER EIGHT

STAFFING THE CHURCH FOR EXPLOSIVE GROWTH

A s the church grows, staffing becomes one of the most important things a pastor does. Finding the right staff who are passionate about the mission of your church and placing them in positions that match their gifts and enhance your DNA (church culture) is a gift that the lead pastor must have or must develop. A mistake here throws out of balance everything else the congregation attempts.

In this chapter we will define staff as both paid and unpaid servants. Both are held accountable to the same standards with the only exception being the amount of time committed. So, we'll use the words *staff* and *servants* interchangeably.

Five Shifts in Staffing

In the past twenty years five shifts have occurred in how churches staff:

- The shift from a professional paid staff who direct volunteers in carrying out programs to paid servants who equip and coach unpaid servants to carry out most of the pastoral responsibilities.
- The shift from using all paid staff to the combination of paid and unpaid servants to fill a role (or part-time paid) or the use of unpaid servants in place of paid staff.
- The shift from the lead pastor seeing the entire congregation

as her or his flock to seeing the key staff positions as his or her flock.

- The rapidly changing climate of our culture has opened the door to the acceptance of a wide variety of different forms of staffing, such as part-time, homegrown, nonprofessionals, bivocational leaders and pastors, team-based leadership, and outsourced consultants. We are seeing more and more laity who have made it financially in life and who devote full-time service to the ministry of their congregation without any payment. [1]
- The shift is from calling seminary trained, ordained, "credentialed" clergy from outside the congregation to raising up most of the leaders from within the church. More on this later.

The Four Primary Roles of Paid Servants

Staff's primary role is to create an environment in which leaders, at every level, are equipped and encouraged to replicate the DNA of the church through living out their spiritual gifts.

Most churches hire staff to "do ministry," and that's why they are in trouble. Staff members should be equippers, not doers. Staff members should never replace unpaid servants; instead, they should create more servants. Staff only do ministry when they are modeling how to do that ministry. Their main task should be to gather and equip teams of unpaid servants for both pastoral and mission ministry. In a biblically based church, staff spend most of their time identifying, inviting, discerning, equipping, deploying, and coaching the church in ministry. Their role is to multiply themselves as many times as possible.

What if every person on your program and pastoral staff identified twenty-five new leaders for the coming year? Would that cause your church to grow? You bet it would. If you have some staff who are doing all of the ministry themselves and never seem to able to find people to equip, either retrain them to be equippers or let them go, and the faster the better.

You should expect the efforts of paid and unpaid servants to result in transformed people who later become so equipped that they can take care of others instead of being cared for by church professionals. A rule of thumb is that most staff who work directly with people should be able to pay for themselves within a year or two through the additional people they attract and equip for service.

The second role of paid staff is to model and add value to the mission statement or core purposes or values of the church. BAF's core value is, "Whatever it takes." Think what that says about how the paid and unpaid staff are going to respond to the challenges of growth. You never hear them say, "It's not in my job description."

A third role of the paid and unpaid staff is to be an extension of the goals of the pastor and congregation. Hopefully these two goals are the same. If they aren't, the church needs to change its goals or get another pastor.

Loyalty to the pastor is as important as loyalty to the congregation. Staff should all complement the pastor's goals as well as fill in the weaknesses of the pastor. No matter how team-oriented a staff may be, if everyone isn't on the same page, the church will never reach its potential.

The body of Christ is like a symphony. Everyone has his or her unique contribution to make, but the orchestra itself is in concert together. Staff should be encouraged to do their ministry their own way, but their view of ministry and vision for the church must be in concert with everyone else on the staff, especially the pastor, if the church is to be healthy. All it takes is for one staff person to be at odds with the mission of the church and energy is drained from everyone.

Finally, the role of the staff is to loyally support all members of the paid and unpaid staff. Most thriving churches have a rule—you can disagree all you want in staff meetings, but in public you can never contradict whatever was decided in a staff meeting; to do so is to be terminated.

The Most Important First Staff Position

After the lead pastor, the first staff person to hire is the worship leader. For some reason many pastors have a hard time seeing the importance of doing whatever you have to do to have someone who can do music and lead worship as well or better than you can preach. We're living in a world where a sermon never reaches its potential without being seamlessly augmented by song and visuals. Even if the lead pastor has these skills, it takes too much time away from the visibility of being in the field.

Listen carefully. Even if you have to take the money out of your own living expenses, find a good worship leader.

When Bil C. was preparing to plant BAF he started praying for someone to do the music. He put feet to the prayers by calling everyone he could think of who might have a lead. He found the future worship leader in another city selling shoes and playing in a band at his church. Bill convinced this person to travel back and forth on the weekends and put a band together for the new church. For eighteen months he made the weekly trip of 100 miles for a whopping $600 a month. As the ministry grew, the pay grew until it was time for the worship leader and his family to move to Corpus and become the full-time worship leader.

What do you look for in a worship leader? Someone who:

- Loves Jesus more than music. (We cannot emphasize this enough.)
- Can pull the talent out of people who don't have much talent. It's not really how much talent the worship leader has but their ability to pull together a team.
- Clicks with the lead pastor as a friend.
- Is on the same mission as you are.
- Is teachable.

The minute you decide a staff person needs to leave, let them go. The longer you wait, the more difficult the transition.

If you have a staff problem, it can actually be the prelude to the growth of your church. Why? Because as painful as firing someone is, you are causing positive change by bringing the right person on your team. You will probably lose some folks who liked the fired staff person, but the passion and skill of the new staff person will far outweigh the loss.

We know you don't like to fire people; we don't either. But the time always comes when you have to do what you don't like to do. If you aren't capable of firing people, you aren't capable of leading explosive growth.

Demonstrated credentials are more important than academic credentials.

Leaders, your ability to lead your church will either thrive or die with your ability to confront ineffective staff, and remove them if they do not change. If the issue is loyalty, you must clear this up, or they need to be removed. If the issue is ineffectiveness, you can typically teach competence if the staff is loyal.

General Staffing Rules

- Pastors need to be responsible for hiring and terminating paid staff rather than a committee. Often, in denominational churches a committee hires and fires staff. Such a practice sets everyone up for failure. Instead, we recommend that either the lead pastor do all the hiring and firing or the process be turned over to an executive pastor or church administrator.
- The most important role a pastor ever does in the large church is to bring the right staff on board and grow them without interference.
- The pastor shepherds the paid staff and key lay leaders rather than the whole church.
- All staff should be equippers rather than doers of ministry. Loyalty to the pastor and to the DNA of the church is a fundamental issue.
- Staff should be hired based on their passion for the mission of the church rather than their expertise or academic background.

- The second most influential paid staff is the worship leader.
- The primary role of all of the staff is to create two cultures: a culture of transformation and leadership.
- As long as we continue to make ordained leaders more important than nonordained leaders we will never be able to staff as effectively from within the church.
- It has always been more productive to hire from within than to go searching on the outside. To grow a staff from within you have to have a farm system in place. See chapter 6.

Staffing the Church from Within

The best way to ensure that the staff team all have the same DNA and are capable of doing what you need done is to hire from within. We've discovered some positive and negative issues of hiring from within.

Positive Advantages of Hiring from Within

You have time to see people with your organization in action so you know they are committed to your mission and what they are capable of doing. The key here is to hire someone who has already proven himself or herself to be an effective team player who can get things done. The staff knows the candidate already and are less likely to have conflict with him or her.

People within your church already have relationships developed within the congregation so the downtime is lessened. When you hire someone from outside, it takes time to establish relationships and trust within the congregation. You avoid this when you hire from within.

You also don't have to advertise to find a candidate, so you save time. It is not unusual for churches that hire from without the congregation to spend upwards of $10,000 to $20,000 in the hiring process.

Disadvantages of Hiring from Within

Some disadvantages are present when you hire from within but they are not nearly as important to note as the advantages.

People from within usually have a lack of specialized training and may require more supervision at first. They also probably lack the fresh ideas they might have if they came from other churches.

They may have too many family relationships within the congregation, making terminating their position a bit more painful. We want to give a strong warning here. Whomever you hire, avoid having a lot of staff from the same family. If you need to fire one of them, while the other is doing good ministry, it is a touchy situation.

Staff Evaluations

We're not believers in lots of paperwork and long sessions when it comes to evaluations. We also don't believe in across the board raises just because someone has finished a year. Both evaluation and salary increases should be tied to one question: did this person significantly add to the value of our mission and is he or she paying their way?

So here is a quick and usable staff evaluation process. At least twice a year, ask each staff person to fill out the following evaluation before the interview and submit it to you a week before:

- What are my most notable achievements so far this year?
- What are the areas in which I have made progress so far this year?
- What are the areas in which I need to make progress before the next evaluation?
- What continuing education or resources do I need to help me add more value to the team? Each staff should be accountable for one week of continuing education that helps him or her further his or her value to the leadership team. They should choose this event, but you should evaluate if they made the right choice.

During the evaluation process week, whoever is responsible for the supervision of that person should fill out the same form for the person being supervised. Then, meet with the staff person and compare his or her evaluation with yours. If staff members do not evaluate themselves the way you have evaluated them, you need to decide if you are both on the same team, if you have not coached them well, or if they just aren't getting it.

Then ask yourself the following questions: *What value is this staff person to our future vision and to the team? Do I like what I see and how can I work with this? Will the team benefit from this person's contribution? If given the chance, would I hire this person again?* Then compare your evaluation with the last four evaluations.

Staff Configurations

There are several models for staff configuration. Each model works well under certain circumstances.

The normal Senior Pastor model requires the following:

- Lead staff report to the lead pastor.
- Lead pastor does the evaluation.
- Lead pastor does the hiring and firing.
- Lead pastor attends and leads all staff meetings.
- Lead pastor directs the day-to-day ministries of the church.

The senior or associate (S.A.) model requires:

- S.A. meets with lead staff weekly and reports to the lead pastor.
- Lead staff report to S.A.
- S.A. does the evaluation with or without the lead pastor.
- S.A. does the hiring and firing.
- S.A. directs the day-to-day ministries of the church.
- Lead pastor is in all combined staff meetings.

The preaching associate model requires:

- This model is the same as the senior associate model except that the pastors share the preaching responsibilities on a weekly basis.

The executive pastor model requires:

- This model is the same as the senior associate model except:
    - The lead pastor probably does not attend the combined staff meeting each week.
    - The lead pastor periodically drops by individual staff members' offices and says, "Tell me what's happening in your ministry and how I can help."
    - The lead pastor must not totally disengage from the staff.

The Fractal Model or Hub Model requires:

- The lead pastor meets with the core team of fractal leaders (four).
- The core fractal team then meets with their second tier fractal, who does likewise, and so on.
- Once a week or monthly, the entire staff, paid and unpaid, get together.
- In some cases, the entire paid staff lunch together weekly. [2]

Common Staffing Mistakes

One common staffing mistake is that pastors too often hire someone because the job needs filling even when they are in doubt of the person's ability to do what is required. It is better to do without staff members than to hire someone whom you will have to let go in a short time.

Another mistake is when a staff member needs to be fired but the pastor delays terminating them even though its obvious the pastor will have to sooner or later. Cut your losses as soon as possible. Even unqualified paid servants build relationships within the congregation. The longer they stay the more relationships they develop. When you let them go, the longer they have been there, the more people are hurt.

Don't have someone on staff who *is* a mission. All staff should be *on* a mission. Many congregations have long-term staff who can no longer function but they keep them because they are "family." As a result, the mission suffers. The kind thing is to help them find a place where they can fill a needed role in the mission. If you have anyone on your staff that is no longer able to grow in their gifts and skills with the growth of the church, we would suggest that you give them a good retirement party or severance package. Staff must be healthy and productive if the church is to be healthy and productive.

Never hire based on credentials. Instead, hire based on passion or gifts or skills.

Hiring associate pastors who function as generalists instead of hiring specialists who are usually nonordained is usually a mistake. In many mainline traditions, associate pastors don't stay long, cost at least twice as much nonordained people, and want to do all of the things the lead pastor does.

The average church in North America makes the decision to hire a youth or student pastor as the first additional staff member. This decision is always a mistake. The reason is simple: *you have more adults than students!* There will come a day when you need to hire a student pastor, and that day is when you can fund a student ministry properly.

One Last Word: Pay Well!

Churches are notorious for trying to hire staff for little or nothing. Let us be as direct here as possible: If you pay peanuts, you get monkeys. When you pay poorly, you will pay in staff turnover and loss of productivity. It will cost you more to not pay well, than to pay well. BAF has a philosophy on paying staff— pay well and expect more work from a slim staff, rather than have a lot of staff who are all starving to death. Make sure your staff is paid at or above market levels for the same position in the same size churches across the country.

A new trend in churches seems to be for the super megachurches to swoop down on the megachurches and hire away their best people. Because of this, team building is critical to ensure loyalty, as is paying well. Both Bills have had staff members offered lucrative positions from "famous" churches and they turned them down. Why? Because when they see the lead pastor turn down those same type positions, they understand the level of loyalty to the long-term vision, and they want to be a part of it. Pay well, it pays the church well. Give a bonus to leaders who do a good job, especially the ones who work hard at preaching and teaching. Scripture tells us, "Don't muzzle a working ox," and, "A worker deserves his pay" (1 Timothy 5:17-18, paraphrased).

If staff is not properly taken care of financially, their family suffers not only the regular burden of ministry, which is sizable at times, but also every struggle is magnified due to a financial struggle. This is not only unfair, it just is plain wrong. When the church takes care of its leaders, its leaders can properly focus on taking care of the church.

Focus Time

- *Do you have any staff who need firing? Why haven't you done it yet?*
- *Do you have a full-time worship leader? If not, what can you do to hire one?*

CHAPTER NINE

SAVED TO SERVE

Have you ever been to a restaurant that offers the best food in town but the service was so bad it didn't matter how good the food was? Bil C. and his wife were told by a number of longtime residents of Corpus Christi that they haven't lived until they tried a certain popular restaurant. So one special date night they went to the restaurant. Were they surprised. It took forty-five minutes just to get a seat. Then they had to wait another forty-five minutes to get their food and that was the last time they saw the waitress until they got the check. The service was so bad that it didn't matter how good the food was. By the time they were served, they were so frustrated they lost their appetite.

People have the same experience in churches. The content of the sermon is amazing. The music is awesome. But the service is so bad that you forget about the great sermon and music—no one helped them park, the nursery smelled, no one said hello—well we could go on but you get the picture.

But, here's something to chew on. The popular restaurant Bil C. and his wife visited is full every night of the week. Why is it still full if the service is so bad? Upon reflection Bil C. realized that the people who recommended the restaurant were longtime residents of the city. They had been going to that restaurant for so long they had become accustomed to poor service. But newcomers like Bil C. and Jessica immediately pick up on the bad service.

Church people make the same mistake. Longtime members don't see the cobwebs in the corners, the stains on the carpet, the smells in the nursery, and are accustomed to bad music. But newcomers are a different story. They notice the cobwebs, the stains, the smells, and they aren't willing to put up with bad music, much less bad sermons. And they won't come back!

So here's the rub. It's one thing to miss a meal at a restaurant; it's a far different matter to miss God's banquet. That's the importance of good service at church. Bad service may cause someone to miss out on God. Service in the church is more important than service at Wal-Mart or at your favorite restaurant.

Christianity has what everyone in the world is searching for. Our message is unbelievably awesome. So why don't newcomers return to most churches? Because most church leaders just won't admit that they provide poor service in their church. But the truth is they don't go out of their way to make the guests feel at home.

Great service allows guests to feel at home and comfortable in their surroundings, and that enables them to pay attention to your message. We don't need to change our content. God's word doesn't need improving. The problem is the people who are supposed to hear the good news aren't there because the week before no one said "hi" to them when they visited, the child care stunk or wasn't even provided, the music was terrible, and the place looked like a wreck. If you're going to use multimedia, it needs to be awesome. If you're going to showcase music, it must be great. If you're going to be a greeter, you need to look presentable and have a smile. If you want parents with children, your nursery better be marked with excellence. That's what God wants to happen in your church—good, great, awesome service to everyone, but especially those first-timers.

Let's look at a few examples of excellence:

- Excellence in worship is making sure that people are greeted five times before walking into the worship service, that there is never more than five seconds where nothing is happening, that the music and graphics are well done.
- Excellence in the nursery is having the nursery close to and on the same level as the auditorium, manned by the same

quality sitter most of the time, with the toys cleaned and the sheets changed in between services, and cribs for every infant, and the infants, toddlers, and walkers separated, and the parents given a pager in case they are needed, or at least a top-notch indication board at the front of the auditorium that is not an interruption to the service.

- Excellence in the children's area means that the environment is conducive to experiencing community and God's love rather then a place to sit and soak. Excellence means your children's church can compete with Disney, and your volunteers fit the image. BAF has rules on appearance in children's areas, making sure that the image of the building and the image of the people match. For example, if you are going for a "Disney feel," you can't have people who look like they are in a rock band leading the children. This is not to say that BAF is opposed to tattoos, wild hair, and black outfits—just not with kids!

- Excellence also means that when it rains, your church has greeters who will run to give an umbrella to someone at their car, and, instead of "sharing it," they give it to the guest and then they (the greeter) runs back in the rain. This sends a loud and clear message that your church cares for visitors.

- Excellence means that if a volunteer is late, we let them know that it is not okay—that people are counting on them. This is not to say that leaders should be "holy drill sergeants," but if there is a pattern of an "I don't care" attitude, you should address it.

- Excellence means that in the music ministry, if someone does not know their part, they should have to wait to perform until they are ready. Also, just because someone likes to sing, does not mean they are given a microphone. Remember, everything you do in your church bears the signature of God—make it excellent.

- Excellence means that your greeters should be handpicked for their friendliness, appearance, and ability to communicate with your target audience. The best way to get a good look and feel in your greeters ministry is to look for people that seem to convey a friendly, warm feeling, or as the Bible says, they have the gift of hospitality (Romans 12:12-14). If people don't come across as warm and friendly they shouldn't be greeters. This is not an elitist attitude, it is simply recognizing that some people want to greet, yet do not come across as they think they do; they are lacking a self-awareness about how they are being perceived. If you have someone who is flirty, they should also be removed because this also sends the wrong message. If you want to reach young families, do you have greeters who match this? If you want to reach singles, do you have single greeters? The first person a visitor wants to see when coming to your church is "themselves." They want to see people just like them, so they know they fit. What impression do your greeters send? Do you even have greeters? Remember, selecting the greeters is not about finding "pretty people," it's about selecting people who make your guests feel welcome while sending a message to them that says "this church is sharp; they know what's up."

Saved to Serve God

One of the basic tenets of Christianity is that Christians are saved to serve. Ephesians 2:8-10 says that we neither make nor save ourselves. God does both the making and the saving. He creates each of us by Christ Jesus to join him in the work he does.

We were saved for a reason and that reason wasn't just so we could go to heaven, much less just sit in a pew. God has things for every Christian to do on behalf of the Kingdom. God wants us to roll up our sleeves and go to work.

And because we were saved to serve, God has prepared us in advance with gifts that match his plan for our life. First Corinthians 12:4-6 says "There are different kinds of gifts, but the same Spirit. There are different kinds of service, but the same Lord. There are different kinds of working, but the same God works all of them in all men" (NIV). Every person has a place of service within the Body of Christ. And when these gifts are linked together with other Christians, the body of Christ is effective. Don't ever think your part is too small or too important. All service is the same with God.

Let's also not forget who we are really serving when we make a guest feel at home. God is really the audience. To paraphrase Matthew 25, "When did we serve you, Lord?" "When you made my creation feel at home in the body of Christ; that's when." When we talk about servants who serve, we aren't just blowing smoke about "involving" them in some activity so they will stay around. We're talking about a foundational biblical principle— the church was meant to be an incubator of faith, a place where people are so engulfed with God's presence and love that they can't help but respond to that love. Such a feeling seldom happens when a church doesn't go out of its way to provide great service to that guest.

Your greatest recruiters of people to serve are those already serving. Ask them to bring their friends and family into the serving team they are on. Empower people, model, and trust them, and they will blow you away with great service.

Service with a Smile

Once Bill E. consulted with a church on starting a third worship service that would be indigenous to its context. In order to do that, it would have to have no more than fifteen minutes in between a traditional worship service and a nontraditional service. Their response to the idea was, "There's no way we could clear out the traditional furniture and bring in the indigenous set in fifteen minutes." Bill E.'s response was, "Do you really mean to tell me if you had five people for every piece that needed to be moved and set up you couldn't achieve that in less than ten minutes?" Their response was, "Sure we could do that; but it would take a lot of people." Bill E. said, "Isn't that wonderful? You would be providing entry level service for new Christians."

Too many churches look for ways to cut down the number of people needed to pull off something. Instead they should see the very act of service to the public as an arena in which those who serve are also being served.

On the other hand, service without a smile, no matter how many people you involve, is worse than no service at all. In many churches all the teams that make up the hospitality teams meet prior to worship service for prayer and reminders of what they are about and the importance of them being frontline people with a smile and a passion to make guests feel at home.

Your attitude when you serve is contagious, for good or for bad. If your hospitality team members have smiles on their faces and go out of their way to be helpful, the guests will catch that positive spirit. But if your team members have scowls on their faces because they are fulfilling a duty and never go out of their way to make the visitors feel like guests in someone's home, the visitors sense this is not a place for them.

So make sure your hospitality team members serve with a smile and live that moment to help a visitor feel at home. Help them see the way in which they provide that service has the potential of making an eternal difference.

Where Does It All Begin

Do you know where your sermon begins? If you have ever been to Disney World, you know the answer to our question. It begins in the parking lot with music, inviting pathways, interestingly named sections of the parking lot, hospitality people roaming around looking for ways to serve with a smile. It isn't long before you know you are a king or queen for the day. Why can't your parking lot say, "Come on in. We're ready for you"?

Visitors form an indelible impression of your church the moment they drive into your parking lot. Bill E.'s parking lot had a sign at every entrance, "First-time guests turn on your lights." The parking lot team would greet them in the parking lot with umbrellas, give them a map of the campus, and show them to the guest parking. All you have to do at BAF is drive into the crowded parking lot and see the eagerness and friendly gestures of the parking crew and the friendly welcome at every door and you know it's going to be a great experience.

Inviting and Experiential

People need to have an inviting experience throughout their time with you. The two key words are *"inviting"* and *"experience."* We live in a time when mediocre and boring are translated by the public into "Run for your life. Don't waste a minute in this place." People need to experience your warmth, grace, and hospitality *before* they can hear and appreciate the content you offer. This type of environment has been dubbed the *"experience econ-*

omy." [1] Businesses like McDonald's and Disney World led the way in this new economy.

> *In 1982 Bill E. had a conversation that changed his outlook on ministry. A young man wanted to be baptized. The problem was he had been baptized as an infant. In Bill E.'s tradition you didn't rebaptize. Finally, after a long conversation, the truth came out. When asked why he was so insistent on being rebaptized he responded, "It isn't real if I haven't personally experienced it!" Bill E. rebaptized him that week. The emerging world began to crystallize with Bill E. that day—we were now living in world in which experience is crucial.*

It is impossible to overstress the importance of the overall experience people have when they attend a church. Everywhere people turn, all of their senses are bombarded by a variety of experiences. To walk into a dull, boring, and unattractive environment is deadly.

Perhaps this sounds silly to you compared to what many Christians are going through in other parts of the world. But we're not there. We live in one of the most electronic and digital environments on the planet. We have to take that into consideration when it comes to what we do when people gather with us.

The experience economy is not going away. If it doesn't entertain, stimulate, and touch all of the senses, it won't educate or be worshipful. Church leaders will have to get over their bias against entertainment if they want to communicate the gospel. Of course, entertainment without the gospel is meaningless. However, it is no more meaningless than many of the worship services we've seen lately.

The word *edutainment* is becoming a common word among clued-in educators. [2] *Sesame Street* began the trend in 1969 when it launched a truly revolutionary method of combining education and entertainment. The trend in children's education continues to become more entertaining with programs such as *Barney* and *Blue's Clues*.

Application Is More Important than Information

Too many churches put so much emphasis on Bible studies and getting people to attend programs that people never get around to actually putting into practice what they are learning. But, application is more important than information. This emphasis on application is one of the big shifts of our time. Psalms 76:11 says, "Do for GOD what you said you'd do—he is, after all, your God" (THE MESSAGE). What a great verse. Do it; don't just talk about it. Actually do it.

For a very long time most of Protestantism's focus has been on getting people to church and participating in some program the church is sponsoring. The emphasis has been on education and learning. We call it "data dumping into the head."

One of Bill E.'s favorite rants is about one of his denomination's most popular and successful programs—DISCIPLE *Bible Study*. This program has had literally hundreds of thousands of people go through it. DISCIPLE *Bible Study* was designed to bring people to the point where they discover their gifts and then go and use them. The problem is that someone decided to create DISCIPLE *Bible Study II* and thousands of people took the second course. Then they waited patiently for DISCIPLE *Bible Study III* and then *IV*. Some are sitting around waiting for version *V*. Each of these courses takes almost a year to complete. So do you get the picture? Some churches have successfully found a way to keep people steeped in dumping and pumping data into their heads and not having time to render service to others. To make matters worse, the material is good and it encourages service, but who has the time to spend two hours minimum a week for thirty-six weeks *and* have any time to serve God? But it gets worse. Some churches promote this madness by telling the flock that what they are doing is a "service" to God.

You can read Scripture all day and memorize tons of Bible verses and be nothing more than satan's cohort. Both know the word, but neither is serving God. It's not enough to have knowledge, because even satan knows the word of God. That's not true discipleship.

True discipleship is serving God through serving others. The highest form of knowledge and learning is application. Too many Christians think that the highest form of learning is memorization. We need to apply good education in the church, and the highest form of knowledge is incarnating God's word in our everyday actions—not just being hearers of the word, but doers of the word.

The early Christians were called "people of the way," not "people of the book." They were on the way with Jesus, out into the world armed with their experience with Jesus. That's what God wants from us today.

Conflict is over when people are equipped to serve and actually serve.

Ephesians 4:11-13 makes it all very clear:

> He is the one who gave these gifts to the church: the apostles, the prophets, the evangelists, and the pastors and teachers. Their responsibility is to equip God's people to do his work and build up the church, the body of Christ, until we come to such unity in our faith and knowledge of God's Son that we will be mature and full grown in the Lord, measuring up to the full stature of Christ.

Let's break these verses down:

- Pastors equip the church for service.
- The people do God's work.
- As a result the church is built up.
- Unity is achieved.

Now you know why so many churches are conflicted and can be compared more to a war zone than an incubator of faith—pastors aren't equipping and the church isn't serving. But if your pastor equips you to do God's work and you do it instead of the pastor doing the ministry, God honors the church with unity and that leads to more people, more spirituality, more walking with God, more love, more prayer, and more honoring of one another.

And if you are applying God's word and it's building up his church and keeping unity with those around you, then your church is maturing in Christ. It will not mature until those things happen.

Commit to Serve and Follow Through

It's not enough for the people just to commit to serve; they must follow through. It's also not enough for the pastor just to equip; he or she has to be willing to coach along the way. We've learned that integrity and trust are developed because people do what they say they're going to do. For people to have integrity when they sign up for service, they show up to serve. That is integrity. Those who are growing in Christ are serving and not just reading about it.

Back to the Restaurant

When you find a restaurant with great service and great food, you know you have a winner. Wild horses can't keep you from returning and bringing your networks with you. And you become a wild-eyed evangelist for the restaurant. Get the picture?

Focus Time

- How often do you preach on the importance of serving?
- Pastor, how much time do you spend each week equipping and coaching your lead staff?
- How would you rate the overall experience on Sunday morning? Poor, Fair, Good, Exceptional, Wow?
- Do you measure success based on how many servants you have?
- Make a list of the areas where you need to improve the quality of your service and

brainstorm with your team on how to improve it.

- *Is there a systematic way of recruiting and equipping people to provide service before, during, and after worship?*

CHAPTER TEN

MAKE A BIG "ASK" OF YOURSELF

Growing a big vision requires raising lots of money. Raising money requires developing a cash flow and multiple streams of income. The key to cash flow is not how much income you have but whether you're spending the income in ways that create the maximum inflow of cash. How you spend the money you have is more important than how much money you have.

We'll tell you up front, the odds are this chapter will push you to your limits. If so, don't be worried; both of us went through the same fear.

The key to making large amounts of money is having multiple streams of income. Money can come from inside and outside of your church. If you are not getting the spiritual results from the dollars you already have, you will not attract donors to give you more. Large donors are sophisticated investors in the kingdom: they want to see your strategy and a proven track record before they will give you large gifts. You must have a way to measure your spiritual results or givers will not take you seriously.

Bil C. confidently asks people for resources because as he puts it, "If you want to change the world, you must take a serious look at investing in this local church. We're changing the world, to the tune of more than 100 people a month receiving Christ." He challenges potential donors, "I challenge you to find a more worthy investment in South Texas that is changing more lives, that is seeing more people find Christ or penetrating the hearts of people that have lost hope." Bil C. is not trying to compare BAF with other churches, but he is trying to gently convince his donors to quit giving to save the whales, and instead help save the people!

Pastor, If You Don't Raise Money for Your Church, No One Else Will

Two-thirds of the way through Bill E.'s twenty-four year ministry at Colonial Hills, a young associate led a young man to Christ who was a millionaire many times over. About a month after his conversion, the young associate came into Bill E.'s office grinning from ear to ear. "Look what I have," he said, laying a $40,000 check on the desk. Bill E. took one look at it and tore it up. Handing the pieces of the check back to the associate he said, "This is like you giving God a dollar bill. Go back to your friend and ask for more." The young associate just about lost it. But a few weeks later he returned. This time he was floating in the air. Without saying a word, he handed Bill E. a check for $400,000 and said, "Now, are you going to tear up this one?" Of course Bill E. didn't and the associate learned a great lesson that day: never let anyone be content with giving God a tip when they could pay for the whole meal.

Bil C.'s story contains more zeros. One Wednesday night during their believer service, Bil C. had just preached on the vision of what God wants to do at BAF, when a friend of Bil C.'s who had made it big and was looking for a way to make a difference in this world said, "Bil, that message moved me. Is there something that I can do for the church? I want to do something." "Yeah, there is," Bil C. said, "You can give us a million dollars." And to Bil C.'s amazement, the man took a step back and said, "I may be able to do that." Six months later he committed a million dollars.

Where did Bill E. and Bil C. find the courage to ask for such large amounts from people? They found it by asking them for ten dollars in the beginning. You see, if you don't make an "ask" of yourself, you never get to asking for the big bucks.

Sure, we can hear you saying, "I can't do that. My denomination wouldn't let me!" We're here to tell you that isn't so. There isn't one denomination on the planet that prohibits its pastors from asking for money. Not one. So, own up to the fact that you need more courage.

Don't delegate raising money to someone else. Others can help, but the lead pastor is the primary fund-raiser. You've got to learn to make a big "ask" of yourself. If you don't learn how to ask, it will never happen. You'll never get 100 percent of the money you never ask for. So you've got to get comfortable asking.

> *"You're going to have to get really comfortable sitting across from people at dinnertime and at lunchtime saying, 'I'm so grateful for the way the Lord has blessed you. And you need to give much of that blessing to the work that we're doing.'"*
>
> *—Ed Young*

And be assured that you are in fine company when you do. One out of every six sentences Jesus spoke was about money. He wasn't afraid to talk about it because he knew it was the last bastion of selfishness among humans. If that was true then, think how much more true it is today.

So you say, "Okay. Let's say I ask for this money and I finally get enough money to get started, then what do I do after that?" You ask for some more. Once the church is up and going, what do you do? You ask for more money. It doesn't matter if you have 50 or 5,000 in worship, you have to ask for money or you don't receive it.

We know you don't want to hear this. We didn't want to hear it either, but we have to do it if we want to grow a big vision into reality. The day you decide to be the primary fund-raiser in your church is the day it becomes possible for God to grow a great vision in your work.

On a side note, if you are going into a major capital fund-raising campaign to buy land or build a new building or expansion, we recommend using a professional capital campaign company. We recommend leaning on their expertise, because just like you look to a general contractor to use his or her expertise to build, so you should use those gifted in raising the funds. They don't make "the ask" for you, but they better prepare you for using the right approach, timing, and strategy. There is a significant difference between what a church raises on its own, versus those who bring in an expert. Very few pastors have successfully navigated a giving campaign without using an outside expert. Humility is big in fund-raising—being willing to admit that capital campaigns are not your expertise makes you teachable, and when you are teachable, God can do some amazing things through you.

If you take us seriously here, you're going to look back in your ministry and realize that almost every advance forward sooner or later involves larger amounts of money.

You can't ignore what we're saying. Anyone can be a pastor or church planter, but it takes a leader to raise the resources to implement that plan. You have to be willing to ask.

To learn to ask takes faith. Such faith doesn't always come easy. Both of us had to get over our fear of making a big "ask" of ourselves. Bill E. had construction in progress twenty times in twenty-four years. That doesn't happen without money. Bil C. is moving BAF into a 2,500-seat auditorium on 100 acres of land, to the tune of millions of dollars. That doesn't happen without money. And that kind of money never materializes unless the lead pastor asks for it.

It takes faith to ask for the kind of money it takes to build a church. Those who never ask, never receive. You have to get comfortable asking people to be good tithers of their income.

Every step of the way has a resource challenge, so you've got to understand that growing a big vision takes a lot of faith to ask. So if we don't have the faith to ask, potential donors are not going to have the faith to give. When you get over your fear of asking for money, they will get over their fear of giving money. Raising money, like everything else in the church, is a faith process.

Money always involves faith. Can you think of a more risky area that requires more faith other than your very own salvation? Money is it. That is why Jesus talked about money and possessions so much—he knew that when you uncover the money issue, the issue underneath it is faith. It is one of the biggest risk areas in the Christian life, let alone in life in general.

But remember God has provided for you in the past and he will continue to do so in the future.

People Give Money to Those Who Ask for It

Do you know whom people give their money to? The answer is to those willing to ask. The people who get the resources, just asked for them.

We want you to think about this. Why is it that churches like Willow Creek and Lakewood can raise all of the money upfront for every one of their building projects and some churches can raise only a portion of the amount? Even Crenshaw Christian Center, located in Watts, burned its note the day they moved in. How can they do this? What's the difference between those churches that just raise cash and those that just raise a portion? One thing—the lead pastor at the beginning of the project said, "We're doing it only in cash." Having said that, the people expect it to happen.

Be Sure to Thank People Personally

Do you know who people give their money to a second time? They give to those who thanked them personally for the first gift. Never deposit a donation until you have said a thank-you. And write that thank-you note that day. That's a good rule to keep because it's too hard to keep up with if you don't. Before you mail in that check, get the name and address off of that check and write a thank-you so when you hand that check to that CPA, your next stop is at the post office to drop the thank-you note. Obviously you cannot do this for every gift given, but make sure you know about the larger gifts in proportion to the giver, and thank them. This may mean a substantial gift of several thousands of dollars, or even several hundred dollars from a struggling single mom or college student. The amount is not the issue, the question is did it take faith to give it.

It All Begins with You Tithing

Pastor, if you don't tithe, you can't ask anyone else to tithe. It's been our experience that too many church leaders don't tithe, including pastors. That's some messed up stuff. Leaders need to not only tithe but give above the tithe.

You may be saying to yourself, "I don't have the money," and you never will until you begin to get honest with your money. But when you begin, God will give you the resources to tithe and beyond. He really will. Begin to tithe and you'll be amazed at what God can do.

Raising Outside Cash Flow

Outside cash flow is money raised outside your church. Churches under 400 or 500 in attendance that want to go beyond survival often need to raise money outside of their church, especially if they are a relatively new church plant. After that size is reached, you don't need to raise money outside anymore. If you do, then there is a teaching problem about money in the church.

Create a Database of Everyone You Know

Start by putting every family member in the database. Don't ask which family member you're not going to include. Put every one of them on it. They may get upset, but do it anyway. You need to put the in-laws and the outlaws on the list also.

Next put your friends and everyone you know on the list. If a name floats into your mind, put it on paper and get his or her address. If people know you, have heard about you, or even hate you, include them in the list. You have to keep in mind that planting or growing this church is a life-and-death matter.

Send Everyone on the List a Monthly Newsletter

Your monthly newsletter should contain a self-addressed stamped envelope with a financial commitment card. All we want to say here is do not include a place for people on your list to say, "No, I can't commit." That's not an option because you really want God to bless them. You may think that sounds a lot like a TV preacher. Well, we hate to break it to you, but most TV preachers get that belief from the Bible. Of course, many have abused it, but it's still a biblical principle. Don't throw away the principle because of the abuses.

Keep mailing the newsletter six months after you are financially self-supported within the church. You want to make sure you really have all that you need. When you stop it you may want to give people the option of being put on your church newsletter list.

If at all possible your newsletter should be quality, full color, and professionally printed. Fill it with spiritual results such as what's going on in the core group (for church planters), how many people are being saved, and why the church needs readers' support. If lives are being changed or if you've got great pictures of your core group or church members or your children's ministries, put them in the newsletter because people want to see where their money is going.

Deliver the Newsletter by the First of the Month

Make sure the newsletter is at everyone's house by the first of every month so that they treat it like a bill and put it in the bill pile. There's a lot of things that you can let slip up. This isn't one of them. This pays your family and keeps your doors open. Okay, so the sermon wasn't that great. So everything didn't come together perfectly in the nursery. This newsletter needs to be there on the first of the month.

Send an immediate thank-you note to those who support you and personally call the largest donors. Make sure they know you appreciate it.

Of course this means that the pastor knows the amount everyone is giving. Let's put to rest the ridiculous notion that the pastor shouldn't know what everyone is giving. That's like your music minister not knowing whether people can sing or your youth minister not knowing any youth. Both of these examples are the equivalent of saying the pastor shouldn't know what everyone gives.

We know what your reservations are at this point. You're afraid that the pastor will cater to the wealthy. Sure, that can happen, but it shouldn't and won't if your pastor is living the right kind of life. Giving preferential treatment to the big givers is not the reason for knowing what everyone gives. If someone writes you a hard-earned check and it's going to affect the way they live that month and you don't personally thank them, you might as well have slapped them in the face.

The first year of BAF a really wealthy person was giving about one-fourth of the total income at the church. That was great until he said, "If you don't start dressing more professionally, I'm out of here." Bil C. said, "Bye."

It's not about preferential treatment of the rich. It's really about two things: first, it's about insuring that no one gets into leadership who has not mastered his or her money. God won't honor that kind of leadership. So someone needs to know what everyone gives. Second, it's about making sure everyone is personally thanked. It doesn't have to be the lead pastor who knows what people give. In many larger churches that task becomes the responsibility of the executive pastor. When someone gives a special gift, the executive pastor can alert the lead pastor to write a note. Or when someone appears to be giving beyond their means it might be necessary to give them permission to reduce their giving.

You see, it's not even about the amount. A single mom writing a check for $200 or $300 deserves a call from the pastor because she has probably made a massive sacrifice.

On the other hand, it's also about holding the wealthy accountable for what God has blessed them with. The best ministry you can have with the wealthy is to confront them about their wealth and God's claim on it; most of the time they will start giving.

Make Those Calls

Make phone calls to churches and individuals to make sure they receive your newsletter, then ask over the phone for their support. The newsletter is the opener for your conversation that will lead to the question of support. It is not a bad idea to have an accountability partner who asks you from time to time if you are making these calls. No one enjoys making them, but they are necessary.

Make sure your newsletter gives a clear presentation of what you're asking for. The newsletter is to tell readers what is going on and why they need to support your ministry. Make sure you do that in every newsletter.

Then, make those calls. And keep making them even when you think you have enough money, keep making those calls. When do you quit raising money? When you've really got all the money you need. Otherwise, you don't quit. You don't get up from the seat until you've called everyone. You've got to have discipline on this one.

Raising Inside Cash Flow

Never delegate asking for money to someone else. Instead, teach on giving in creative ways. Share the vision and then ask for financial backing to make it happen. Never just ask for money. Ask people to support the vision. Churches with no vision ask people to pay light bills or phone bills. Pastors with God's vision talk about changing the world, and that takes money. You've got to tie the vision to the resources.

> *Never focus fund-raising on money. Focus it on the vision of what God is doing and can do if people give.*

A money problem is really a vision problem; either you don't have a compelling vision or you're not sharing it effectively or there's a trust issue with your people. Remember:

- Be bold enough to ask again and again.
- Be honest about your needs. People may think you're doing okay when your church is actually starving.
- Bring a fresh new vision of growth to your people and ask them to give to the vision and the new vision budget.
- Pray like never before.
- Ask your people to pray for the resources to go BIG as a church.
- Study the great communicators and how they ask for money. Order tape sets of their giving campaigns. If you're not taking advantage of what they've learned, you're crazy. They become your personal research assistants. You don't have to agree with everything someone says to be able to use their resources.
- Never let your first giving campaign be for a building. Make your mistakes on a smaller scale when the stakes are not so high.

Consider this: one of Bil C.'s church planters asked about his financial struggles and what to do. Bil suggested that he take a six pack of his favorite cola, and stack them onstage and place a creative sign above them with the title of an outreach vision that costs, say for example, an extra $12,000 above the regularly needed budget. Then, on a specific weekend, speak on the vision of reaching people through the new outreach ministry, maybe including some advertising through whatever media is good in your community. Then put the price of $1,000 per can on each can and stack the cans in a creative way onstage. Challenge your people to buy a $1,000 can towards the vision and keep bringing it up each week at the end of the service until all cans are paid for, and then you can do your outreach campaign. You will be amazed at how fast the cans will sell once people get the vision.

At the time of this writing, the church planter is doing this with great success. This is not a new idea—leaders have been doing this kind of fund-raising in and out of the church for years, because it works. The more creative you get in fund-raising, the more people will respond. Try to make giving fun.

Never Guilt People into Giving

Instead of playing on people's guilt, tell them the benefits of investing in your church. Share personal testimonies, live or by video, of people who are giving and what it means to their everyday Christian walk. Ask them to tell what God is doing in their life. Most people want to give, but they are scared to let go until they see someone else give a testimony about how giving is working out for them. And then people think that "if they can do it, I can do it."

Both Bil C. and Bill E. made this promise to people every year: "If you've never tried tithing, then do so for three months and if your life isn't changed for the better, we'll return your money 100 percent." Guess what? Neither has ever had to return the money.

Bil C. keeps a folder of all the e-mails and letters that testify to amazing things that God has done financially in their lives. When someone says, "I'm just scared to tithe," Bil C. asks them to go through the folder and read the testimonies.

Those Who Don't Give Aren't Committed

No matter how vocal a person is about their commitment to your church, if they aren't giving a tithe, they aren't committed. They can be as vocal as they want but they're not in the boat. Jesus told it like it is: "For where your treasure is, there your heart will be also" (Matthew 6:21 NIV). And so just know where our hearts are. If one of your staff doesn't tithe, warn the person. If he or she doesn't change, fire them. If one of your leaders isn't tithing, ask them to step down until they are willing to tithe.

Don't be afraid to hold people accountable. Too much is at stake to do anything else. Reaching the world is worth the cost of asking for money, so get over your fear.

We Hope You Get the Message

Never shy away from asking for money because you're asking for the greatest mission in the world—God's mission to save creation. You should never be embarrassed. The one who should be embarrassed is the one who refuses to give! As a leader, if you allow finances to hold your church back from reaching your community, then you just allowed finances to become your God. Think about it and go make an "ask" of yourself.

Focus Time

- *Do you give to God 10 percent of your gross or net income? If not, what is standing in your way? Make a list. Are any of the reasons more important than the mission?*
- *Do all of your leaders tithe? If not, do you ask them to step down until they do?*
- *Do you personally thank people who make any form of sacrificial gift?*
- *If you are a church planter, take the time to make your lists of networks and send out that newsletter at the first of each month.*
- *Start keeping a folder of all of the testimonies you receive about how God has blessed your people.*
- *Are you making a big "ask" of yourself? If not, are you ready to begin now?*

CHAPTER ELEVEN

HANDLING PROBLEM PEOPLE

S ooner or later even the best of churches encounter problem people. Problem people come in all shapes and sizes,
but they all have one thing in common—they cause a dis-
ruption within the body that, if not addressed, greatly dimin-
ishes the effectiveness of the church's ministry. An effective
leader knows that too much is at stake to let anyone disrupt
the mission.

If you're not ticking off someone, your vision is either too
broad or too small or nonexistent. In other words, leaders with
vision always have their detractors who take issue with them.
That is a natural part of leadership. If this reality bothers you,
your leadership will be diminished because a good leader gives
loyalty to and expects it from everyone in the church.

*Every church experiences problem people now
and then. The best practice is to show them the
door ASAP, because the odds are they will never
change. Some church has groomed them to be
this way by allowing them to get away with
murder. Don't you dare make the mistake of tol-
erating problem people, or it will come back to
haunt your ministry.*

Never allow problem people to cause you to take your eyes off the priorities God has given you. The greatest danger is not the problem people but how you allow them to affect your leadership. The more they affect your leadership the less your church will help fulfill the Great Commission. When opposition arises, and it will, let it be the catalyst that causes you to focus on your priorities even more. Remember the scripture here—"Do not answer a fool according to his folly, / or you will be like him yourself". (Proverbs 26:4 NIV).

Handle Problem People Quickly, Directly, Lovingly, and Firmly

Never allow a problem person to have any room. Once it is apparent they are a liability to your mission, deal with them quickly, directly, lovingly, and firmly. The longer you put it off, the more of a problem they will become. Warn them once and if they don't change ask them to leave. It's that simple. We are encouraged in Titus 3:10, "Warn a quarrelsome person once or twice, but then be done with him" (THE MESSAGE). If they leave, let them, and by all means don't feel as if you have to ask them to return. That's the height of foolishness.

Confront the Bullies

Most struggling churches are held hostage by one or two bullies or controllers who are opposed to the church making any radical change, even if the change would give the church a chance to thrive once again. These persons get their sense of self-worth by keeping the church so intimidated, either by their actions or their money, that very little can happen without their approval. The sad thing is most of the leaders know that these persons are a stumbling block to the church's future but they won't do anything about it. They don't confront the bully because they think that is the "Christian" thing to do, and in so doing, assist in the stunted growth or death of the congregation.

When confronted with such people our advice is either to convert them, neutralize them, or kick them out. Proverbs 22:10 tells it to us straight: "Drive out the mocker, and out goes strife; / quarrels and insults are ended"(NIV).

The body cannot live with such cancer. Mature Christians care so deeply about advancing the kingdom that they will do anything, even not being nice, *for the sake of the gospel.*

> **Remove the few bullies and the church has a chance to grow.**

Now we can just hear the cries, *"That's not very Christian!"* You think not? We think you have confused being nice with being Christian. Too many church leaders believe that it is more important to be nice than *Christian,* and teach that the essence of Christianity is to be nice. Where do we get such a notion? Certainly not from the actions of Jesus.

Follow the Example of Jesus

One of the hallmarks of Jesus' ministry was his constant attack on the status quo. He challenged it every time he could. He even went out of his way to upset the religious bullies of his time (see, for example, Matthew 12). Jesus loved people too much to allow them to remain such small persons. Being nice has nothing to do with being Christian. Being nice is often nothing more than a lack of compassion for people.

Jesus shows us what to do with people who do not want to grow spiritually. In training his disciples how to spread the word of God's love, he told them to shake off the dust of their feet when they encountered people who did not receive them graciously (Matthew 10:14). Jesus loved people too much to let anything slow down the process of advancement of the kingdom of God.

And who can forget that fateful day when Jesus met the money changers in the temple. Remember what he did? In a holy rage, he entered the temple with a whip and drove them out (Matthew 21:12). We wouldn't call that very nice.

People who would rather be nice than Christian do not love enough. They do not have enough compassion. Instead, they are afraid of hurting someone or of being hurt. Fear is the opposite of love. Remember, "Perfect love drives out fear" (1 John 4:18 NIV).

If your church isn't growing, the odds are you have one or two bullies in your midst and before renewal happens you are going to have to deal with them and it won't be nice. Just make sure your actions are Christlike. And remember, not even Jesus got through the journey with all of his disciples. Why should we expect to?

This does not mean that we should set out to intimidate the bully or to kick people out of the church. But it does mean that we care enough about the future of our church not to allow anyone to stifle its ability to liberate people from bondage or victimization. It means that we care enough about the bully that we will not allow the bully to intimidate the church because we know the spiritual vitality of both the bully and the church is at stake.

Apply Matthew 18 to the Bully

Matthew 18 gives us a formula for dealing with the bully. First, an individual privately confronts the person with what he or she is doing and asks the person to stop. If this doesn't achieve positive results, two or more people are to confront the person. If this does not resolve the matter, the person is to be brought before the entire church. Listen again to the *not-so-nice* words of Jesus. "If he refuses to listen to them, tell it to the church; and if he refuses to listen even to the church, treat him as you would a pagan or a tax collector" (Matthew 18:17 NIV). In other words, withdraw from that person's presence, or remove that person from office! Never, ever, allow such a person to dictate the direction of the church.

The next time someone in your church attempts to intimidate or bully the church out of taking a positive step forward, go to God in prayer, and then get out the "whip" and drive that person out of the church—of course in love. [1]

Never Take Criticism Personally

You are the spiritual barometer in your church. If you overreact to criticism or blow it out of proportion, so will the church. Don't get mad if someone comes directly to you and says they were offended or upset about something that was said. Be grateful they came directly to you, and be humble, because they may be right. When they are, apologize sincerely.

Bill E. is fond of saying "no one has ever been mad at me." Of course if you know Bill E.'s style, you know that isn't true. What he means by that statement is that when people get mad at church it is usually some form of transference of something going on at home or at work. They're not mad at him or the church, they're just mad. When you approach criticism this way, you avoid over-reacting and causing the problem to escalate.

Never Get Discouraged over a Loss

Moses didn't get everyone to Canaan and Jesus didn't get through to all of the disciples. So why should you be any different? You will lose people along the way. Some of them may even have been your best friends. That's life; get over it for the sake of the gospel.

Pastor People on Their Way Out

Bil C. tells people who continually complain about church that they should seriously pray about whether Bay Area Fellowship is the church God called them to. Bil has many times admitted when he has erred; however, when someone continues to complain about the way he "does church," he will remind them that church is a volunteer place to be; no one is forcing them to attend a church in which they are "so miserable."

He often uses this illustration. Suppose someone were to go to a movie, and they did not like it. They may leave, and even tell a friend or two, why that movie was not for them. It is certainly acceptable to have an opinion. However, wouldn't it be foolish to then return to the same movie the next week, lean over in the middle of it, and begin trying to convince the other people attending the movie that the movie is bad? Bil C. then simply says, "It's okay not to like the movie, but don't ruin the experience for someone else who does want to be there. That's not only having an opinion, that is selfishly sharing it to hurt the 'cause' of the movie, or in our case 'the cause of Christ.'"

Common Criticisms

Some of the most common criticisms you will hear from people leaving a church are:

- **The message isn't deep enough.** This means "the message is not my style," or it could mean the person is confusing his or her personal quiet time with corporate worship. It could also mean that you have a person who listens to Christian radio all day, or watches Christian television constantly, so they are comparing you with the best of the best preachers in America, which is unfair to anybody. Bil C. used to get paranoid, thinking he wasn't a good enough preacher, until he heard Dr. Charles Swindoll say that the number one reason people leave his church is because the person exiting says, "You're not deep enough."

- **The pastor is not accountable.** The first thing you must do with this response is genuinely ask yourself, "Am I accountable? Have my actions merited a checkup with my accountability?" This can be legitimate, but far too often it's not. Have you ever noticed how the person saying you are not accountable never questioned this issue until you made a decision they personally did not like? Most people who complain about you not being accountable are really saying "you are not giving *me* control." Trust us—let them go. If they desire to stay and cause problems, ask them to leave. But one warning: when they leave, there will two or three families who will go with them, because as one leader said on this issue, "Wolves run in packs."

- **The church is getting too big.** If someone is upset over this, tell them they will be miserable in heaven! There's a whole lot of people there! This one is so selfish, you just need to call it what it is—a blatant disregard for the unsaved in your community.

The Advantage of Problem People

If it were not for problem people, you would not be the forged leader you are today. Also, you would probably not pray as fervently, and most important, you might not discover your future team.

When someone is walking out on you, practice this exercise. Ask God to show you who is defending you. Those are your future "go to" impact players. Hire them! Let me say this again: Hire them! Both Bill and Bil have experienced a high level of loyalty, because they give it and receive it. Loyalty is not really known until problem people come along and test it.

The Last Word

The real danger of problem people is when you give them the ability to make you doubt your own leadership. They will make you feel as if you are wrong if you don't do what they want. Don't listen to them. Instead, remember when you were called to start, or go to that church. Did God call you? If so, then remember your calling never included other people's opinions. Trust the leadership God put in you. If your biggest fans question you, then by all means, stop and look at what you are saying, because those people love you.

You may be having a problem with this chapter. If so, you probably have a high mercy gift. By that we mean you really have trouble with people not liking you or with confronting people concerning their inappropriate behavior. You prefer to avoid conflict and sweep the problem people under a rug hoping they will change. Trust us—such behavior never works and never grows a church, much less explosively grows a church.

Here are three things to ask yourself to see if you have a high mercy gift:

- Do I need people to like me?
- Do I find it next to impossible to fire a staff member or ask a problem person to leave the church?
- Do I avoid dealing with controversy?

If you answer any one of these yes, then you probably have a high mercy gift.

If you sense a high mercy gift is standing between you and the growth of the kingdom, then do one of three things: one, work on developing your leadership skills and consciously going out of your way to lessen your drive for mercy. Two, hire a Jethro who can do the hard confrontational stuff for you. Often this is

123

impossible in the small church. Three, find a place on a church staff where your strong mercy skills are needed but don't try to be a lead pastor.

Focus Time

- The last time a problem person acted out at your church, how did you handle it? Do you feel good about it? If so, why? If not, why? What did you learn about yourself?
- If you are having trouble confronting problem people, perhaps you need to see if your mercy gift is high. Have you spent any time learning how your personality functions? Try taking a spiritual gift inventory or one of the more reputable personality tests to see how high or low your mercy gift is.

CHAPTER TWELVE

POSITIONING OURSELVES FOR EXPLOSIVE GROWTH

We unashamedly speak of explosive growth in this book (and in a planned series of books to follow) because that is the blueprint we find throughout the Scriptures. We have focused most of your attention on the role of the lead pastor because as goes the lead pastor so goes the church. For explosive growth to happen in a church, it is absolutely essential for the lead pastor to have the freedom and the accountability to be the spiritual and administrative leader of the entire congregation. If the lead pastor isn't dreaming a big picture and positioning the church to receive an outpouring of God, explosive growth never happens. So what do you need to do, Pastor, to get ready for explosive growth?

What Is to Come

But as we said, one of the keys to explosive growth is keeping those who show up. So our next three books will be focused on the three areas of the church that must function with excellence—small groups, children's ministry, and worship.

To whet your appetite, here is the outline for the next book in the series (tentatively titled *Go BIG: Small Groups that Change Lives*):

Keys to a Healthy and Growing Small-Groups Ministry in Your Church

1. **Commitment and support from the top leadership:** church board, senior pastor, and so on.
2. **Strong Ministry Leadership:** Someone to cast and carry out the vision for the ministry. This person must be relentless if they plan on growing a small-groups ministry in a fast-growing church (small groups pastor, director, leader, and so on).
3. **Multiplication:** Small-group leaders with a passion for growth and multiplication who understand their role in achieving that goal. Leaders who can and will reproduce their leadership in others—not once but many times.
4. **Training:** A system of training that will prepare leaders to support the vision of a growing and multiplying small-groups ministry.
5. **A Program for success:** A system of management and support to keep the ministry growing and healthy.
6. **Vision:** A vision of where the ministry is heading and how it is going to get there.
7. **Goal:** Some ridiculously huge goal that only the *right leaders* would even consider possible.
8. **Plan:** A well-thought-out plan for how to get as many people in your church as possible to join small groups once you have them.
9. **Prayer:** Recognizing that none of the above is possible without God.

Our Prayer for You and Your Church

Throughout this series our prayer for you and your church is, "God position these spiritual leaders for an awesome demonstration of your power as seen before in the Acts of the Apostles and as is being seen all over the world today."

Bil and Bill

2. A Wild and Crazy God

1. Malcolm Gladwell, *The Tipping Point: How Little Things Can Make a Big Difference* (New York: Little, Brown and Company, 2000).
2. For more on the call and its importance, see Bill Easum, *Put On Your Own Oxygen Mask First* (Nashville: Abingdon Press, 2004).

3. Structuring Your Church for Growth

1. For more on the relationship between a strong leader and a team-based environment, see Bill Easum and Dave Travis, *Beyond the Box* (Loveland, Colo.: Group, 2003).
2. For more on this, see Easum and Travis, *Beyond the Box*.

4. It's Time to Lead, Pastor!

1. For more on setting your own agenda, see Easum, *Put On Your Own Oxygen Mask First* (Nashville: Abingdon Press, 2004).

5. Double Your Vision

1. Some of the better church marketing firms are Outreach Marketing, out of California, and Manlove Advertising or Lakesound, out of Texas.
2. Bay Area Fellowship uses Video Marketing, an independent advertising firm run by Jimmy Kuddes, (361) 808-9812.
3. For more information on taking a gift to first-time visitors, see "Evangelism in Traditional and Non Traditional Churches" at our Web site. http://easumbandy.com/store/shop/EBA_store.html?state=search& cartid=5771becf60fb74039090dccb0b09e8d3.

6. Preparing to Break the Growth Barriers

1. For information on what these initiatives might be, see Bill Easum, *Unfreezing Moves* (Nashville: Abingdon Press, 2001).

7. The Growth Barriers

1. You can find message content from Bill Easum at www.easum bandy.com, or Bil Cornelius at www.bayareafellowship.com.

2. See Lyle E. Schaller, *The Very Large Church: New Rules for Leaders* (Nashville: Abingdon Press, 2000).

3. For more on multiple sites, see Bill Easum and Dave Travis, *Beyond the Box* (Loveland, Colo.: Group, 2003).

4. See Bill Easum, *L.I.F.E. Groups.* This is a workbook for setting up a small-group system from Easum, Bandy & Associates that Bill Easum used during his ministry. Go to http://www.easumbandy.com/store/shop/EBA_store.html?state=search&cartid=098e19adae0221ebf16ee6fc3ae7c454.

5. See Wayne Cordeiro, *Doing Church as a Team* (Ventura, Calif.: Regal Books, 2001).

6. The groups of twelve model is being tested in the U.S. by Bethany World Center in Baker, Louisiana and the Church of the Nations in Athens, Georgia.

7. For more see Bill Easum, *Sacred Cows Make Gourmet Burgers* (Nashville: Abingdon Press, 1995).

8. See Bill Donahue and Russ Robinson, *Walking the Small Group Tightrope* (Grand Rapids: Zondervan, 2003); and M. Scott Boren, ed., *Small Group Ministry in the 21st Century* (Loveland, Colo.: Group, 2003); and www.smallgroups.com.

8. Staffing the Church for Explosive Growth

1. Before Bill E. left the local church in 1993 to become a consultant, his church had two full-time, unpaid servants working on the staff.

2. For more on the fractal model, see Easum, *Unfreezing Moves,* or Wayne Corderio, *Doing Church as a Team* (Ventura, Calif.: Regal Books, 2005).

9. Saved to Serve

1. B. Joseph Pine II and James H. Gilmore, *The Experience Economy: Work Is Theatre & Every Business a Stage* (Cambridge: Harvard Business School Press, 1999).

2. See http://edu.kde.org/, http://www.familyfirst.com/the_edutainment_catalog.html.

11. Handling Problem People

1. For more on how to do this, see William M. Easum, *Sacred Cows Make Gourmet Burgers* (Nashville: Abingdon Press, 1995).